KW

K

ANCIENT MYSTERIES

Peter Haining

Hutchinson of Australia

Sidgwick & Jackson

ACKNOWLEDGEMENTS

For
WILLIAM ARMSTRONG
publisher and friend

The author is grateful to those listed below for supplying material for use in this work, and for permission to reproduce; to Mrs Pamela Scott for typing the manuscript and to Jane Heller for tireless editorial work throughout the whole project.

Ashmolean Museum, page 66; Associated Press, 132–3; Australian News and Information Bureau, 36 top and bottom, 37 top, 41 bottom; Black Star, 166 top right, 170 top; Bodleian Library, 93; British Museum, 44–5, 72–3, 74–5, 75 bottom; British Tourist Authority, 69 top, 86 bottom, 87 bottom; Camera and Pen International, 82–3 top and bottom, 83 top; Camera Press, 155 bottom; J. Allan Cash, back cover, inset bottom right, 58–9, 62–3 top, 68 top, 68–9 bottom, 103 top; Conway Picture Library, 141 inset; *Cork Examiner*, 47; René Dahinden, 130–1 bottom; *Daily Mail*, 166 bottom left; *Daily Mirror*, 154, 166 centre bottom; *The Field* (by courtesy the owner, David James M.P.), 148; *Flying Saucer Review*, 166 top left and centre right, 166–7 bottom (photo: Howard Menger), 168 bottom, 171 (photo: Howard Menger and G. W. Tassel); Gilcrease Museum, Tulse, 53 bottom right; Rupert T. Gould, 143 top left and top right, 156 left, 156–7; Gresham Publishing Co. Ltd., 120–1; Hugh Grey, 142–3 bottom; Michael Grumley, 133 top; *Harper's Monthly Magazine*, 94; Harry Price Library, 28 bottom, 42, 108 bottom left, 117; Icelandic Tourist Information Bureau, back cover, bottom left, 2, 90–1; *Illustrated London News*, 96–7, 123, 124 top and bottom, 124–5, 127 top and bottom, 144–5, 152–3 top, 153 centre; *Inverness Courier*, 140; Mansell Collection, 87 top, 89; National Film Archive, 14; *New Orleans Item*, 163 top; *New York Times*, 12 bottom left and right; *Observer*, 26; Roger Patterson, 130–1 top; Photographers International (photo: Terry Fincher), 139, 141, 155 top; Picturepoint, 40–1 top, 104; Popperphoto, back cover, top, 17 top, 30–1 top, 103 bottom, 158–9, 164–5 top and bottom; Robert Harding Associates, front cover, 35, 39; Royal Society of London, 12–13; Ivan T. Sanderson, 113 bottom, 126–7; Soviet Press Agency, 109 bottom right; *Sunday Times*, 134; Theosophical Society, 5, 84–5; *Time* magazine, 157 top; Transworld Feature Syndicate (photo: Hamish MacInnes), 27 bottom; U.S. Government Archives, 19 top and bottom; U.S. Government Environmental Science Service Administration, 8 top, 9; Robert Wilson, 146; Zürich Central Library, 160–1 top. The diagram at the bottom of page 17 was drawn specially for this book by Christopher Scott.

FRONT COVER: The statues on Easter Island.
BACK COVER: *Top left*: George Adamski's famous photograph of a Flying Saucer taken in California in December 1952; *Top right*: Sir Peter Scott's painting of two Loch Ness Monsters; *Centre left*: Mummified body, found in Central America, of what is believed to be a Second Race man; *Centre right*: One of the strange cave paintings in the Kimberley Ranges, Australia; *Bottom left*: The island of Surtsey; *Bottom right*: Geometrical plan of Stonehenge, an illustration from William Stukeley's *Stonehenge: A Temple Restor'd to the British Druids* (London 1740); *Inset bottom right*: The Dromara Dolmen in Northern Ireland.

Page 1: The Ancient World – a seventeenth-century woodcut taken from *The Discovery of America by Northmen* by N. Beamish, published in New York 1841

Page 2: The emergence of the island of Surtsey

First published in Great Britain in 1977

Copyright © 1977 by Peter Haining and Sidgwick and Jackson Limited

Designed by Graham Mitchener

Hutchinson Group (Australia) Pty Ltd
30–32 Cremorne Street, Richmond, Victoria, 3121
London, Melbourne, Sydney, Auckland
Wellington, Johannesburg and agencies
throughout the world

Printed in Spain by Printer industria gráfica s.a. Barcelona D.L.B. 92-1984

ISBN 283 98321 3

CONTENTS

A modern impression of a
'second race' man

INTRODUCTION

IT WAS Oscar Wilde, that splendid Victorian *littérateur* with a genius for summing up, who wrote in 1891, 'Nowadays we have so few mysteries left to us that we cannot afford to part with one of them.' He undoubtedly sensed that the enormous strides being made in scientific progress were leading to a twentieth century during which the foundations of many beliefs held for generations were to be shaken if not actually demolished, and traditionally accepted viewpoints vigorously opposed. The world, as Wilde knew, was in for a shake-up, and he was not sure where it might all lead.

As we journey into the last quarter of the twentieth century, with space travel an actuality and science the master of problems that defied previous centuries, we can see that Wilde's appraisal was not far wrong. We certainly don't have as many mysteries as we did a hundred years ago; but far from parting with certain of those remaining to us, we have begun to re-examine them with all the accoutrements of science and learning now at our disposal, and with our speculative powers much increased. Whether we are going to like – or accept – what we find, only time will tell.

In the past year or so, this re-examination of ancient mysteries has become a subject of great interest not only among scientists, but among laymen as well. A host of books and speculative writings has been published proposing wholly new approaches to the stories of ancient civilizations said to have flourished at the dawn of time; strange creatures believed to dwell on the borderlands of civilization; the real purpose of stone edifices and huge buildings erected during the infancy of mankind; and new theories about the possibility of the earth being hollow, about the existence of a 'Second Race' of human beings living in secret, and what the mission of those strange aerial phenomena known as flying saucers might be.

Because this wholesale reappraisal of our ancient mysteries is still such a new development, it has led to strikingly divergent attitudes, not to say bitter argument and controversy at all levels. To my way of thinking, all these extreme viewpoints miss the essential importance of such a development: and this is that we are at last prepared to look at the past with fresh eyes, refusing to be bound by centuries of tradition. We must not overthrow for the sake of overthrowing, of course, but the importance of the books of people like Charles Fort, Immanuel Velikovsky, Erich Von Daniken and their colleagues depends less on the general acceptability of their theories than on the fact that they are opening up new areas of research and thought. It was not so long ago, remember, that people went to the gallows or were burnt at the stake as heretics for questioning the accepted truth, whether it was right or wrong.

Already, as I have said, this new speculation has produced a veritable library of books and papers – of varying levels of scholarship and propounding a wide variety of theories. What we haven't yet got is a general survey of the most important 'ancient mysteries', the facts about them, and the latest speculations concerning them; in other words a 'reader' or first guide for the person interested in the subject, neatly packaged in one volume. That is what I have tried to achieve with this work.

Because of the worldwide nature of ancient mysteries and the impossibility of doing justice to them all in a single volume, it was felt advisable to concentrate mainly on those belonging to the English-speaking peoples – the British, Americans, Canadians and Australians – but also including certain others, such as Atlantis or the Abominable Snowman, which although not native to the English-speaking world have undoubtedly fascinated it. Apart from sketching in the historical background of each of the mysteries, I have also tried to mention the more important theories concerning them. The pictures, too, have been selected not only because they can often speak more eloquently than a thousand words, but because they frequently highlight some major school of thought or theory relating to the subject in question. Unfortunately, of course, it would be quite impossible to cover every ancient mystery even within the English-speaking world, but the major ones are certainly here and the path to others lies clearly indicated.

The reader is going to find, just as the author did in his research, much in these pages that is amazing, startling, perhaps even unbelievable. For these are topics as challenging to the mind in their possibilities as the thought of space travel was to the people of Oscar Wilde's time. When we are tempted to think that we have advanced so far that there must really be very little we don't know or can't explain, it is worth remembering that we are not even sure of such a basic thing as how long man has been on earth. Certain scientists have suggested that our world was ready for man *at least* fifty million years before his earliest known appearance. With such a likelihood before us, who can say what exciting worlds possibly still await our investigation?

Peter Haining
February 1976

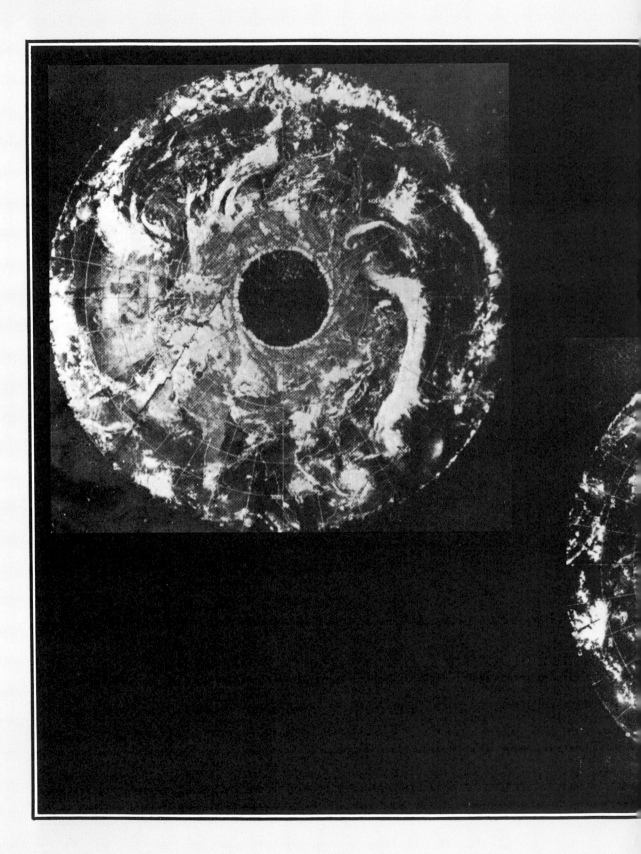

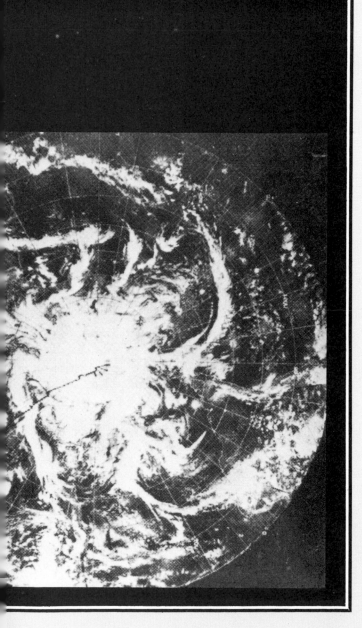

THE
HOLLOW
EARTH

These two photographs of the North Pole were
taken by an American space satellite on 23
November 1968. The photograph on the left
indicates that there is a hole in the North Pole;
the picture on the right gives a more traditional
view of the Pole – shrouded in cloud

PROBABLY the oldest and most intriguing mystery that has perplexed mankind concerns the very ground on which we live – is our earth a solid mass or a hollow sphere containing a secret world beyond our understanding? It is an issue that has absorbed scientist and layman alike, and presented both with many fascinating possibilities and unanswered questions. There could, in fact, be no more appropriate subject with which to begin a book such as this.

The earth, which is an oblate spheroid, has a circumference at the equator of 24,902 miles, and a surface area of 197 million square miles, of which over 70 per cent is covered by water. According to the most widely accepted theory, it is thought to consist of a small inner core of solid iron and nickel (about 800 miles wide), an outer core of molten iron and nickel, a mantle of solid rock (1,800 miles thick), and on top of this the three-to-five-mile covering of the outer crust. Conversely, according to those who have claimed that the earth is hollow, inside the crust there is a world of oceans and land masses, entered by way of a vast network of subterranean tunnels. Others of this mind have in recent years affirmed that there are giant holes at both the North and South Poles – usually obscured by cloud – which also lead to the inner world.

Belief in this theory is no modern aberration, however, for it can be traced back to antiquity. Plato, for instance, wrote about 'tunnels both broad and narrow in the interior of the earth' which led eventually to 'enormous subterranean streams'.[1] He wrote, too, of the 'God who sits in the centre, on the navel of the earth', and this is a phrase to be found repeatedly in early literature. The Bible also has references which it has been maintained refer to an inner world. In the Book of Job we find, 'He stretcheth out the north over the empty place, and hangeth the earth upon nothing,' and in Ephesians, 'Now that he is ascended, what is it but that he also descended first into the lower parts of the earth?'

Ancient Buddhist doctrine teaches of a subterranean world called Agharta where millions of people live in an underworld paradise ruled over by the all-wise Rigden-jyepo, the King of the World, who dwells in the capital city Shambala. This deity is also said to influence the activities of those who live on the surface world, and messages are relayed to and from him by a group of monks who travel the secret passages linking the underworld to ancient Buddhist monasteries.

Opposite: 'The Central Sea', an illustration from an 1876 edition of Jules Verne's *A Journey to the Centre of the Earth*

Even when one passes out of the age of fable and legend into the Dawn of Reason, the Hollow Earth theory is still being propounded, but now receives more scientific support. In 1692, the Astronomer Royal of England, Dr Edmund Halley, who gave his name to probably the most famous of all comets, affirmed his conviction in an address to the Royal Society of London. 'Beneath the crust of the earth,' he said, 'which is 500 miles thick, is a hollow void. Inside this space are three planets. They are approximately the size of Mars, Venus and Mercury.'[2]

At the beginning of the eighteenth century, Leonard Euler, the Swiss academician and one of the founders of higher mathematics, also lent his formidable weight to the idea, but he disagreed with Halley's notion of there being three planets in the interior. He maintained there was just one central sun which provided daylight for a highly advanced civilization. Another mathematician, the Scotsman Sir John Leslie, also speculated on the idea later that same century, and, partially as a result of his work on radiation, declared that there were two suns inside the earth, and named them Pluto and Proserpine.

Another man who entered the debate, but who had no particular beliefs as to the number of suns, was the American clergyman Cotton Mather. Unfortunately his reputation as a philosopher and his conviction of the 'hollow world beneath our feet'[3] were overshadowed by the religious fanaticism which he showed during the persecution of suspected witches at Salem in 1692.

Nevertheless it was to be a fellow American who did most to publicize the Hollow Earth theory just over a hundred years later. He was Captain John Cleves Symmes, a brave and inspired soldier who was decorated for his part in the war against England in 1812–14. He was, though, a man given to outbursts of temper and prone to insubordination: and this led to his being

assigned to isolated posts after the hostilities had ceased. Symmes put this time to good use by reading up on the subject which increasingly fascinated him – the constitution of the earth. When he had absorbed all the related published material, he formulated his own theory and announced with passionate conviction that 'The earth, and the other planets, are hollow. There are five concentric spheres inside the outer surface. This is like five globes placed one inside the other. They have a common centre.'[4]

In making his proposal, Symmes agreed that he defied Newton's theory of gravity ('Objects on Earth', he maintained, 'are subject for their movement to an aerial plastic fluid invisible to the eye'[5]), but proposed to prove everything by resigning his commission and setting up an expedition to the inner world. In May 1818 he sent an appeal to all the most influential people in America – including members of the government – and to several heads of state abroad. It read:

LIGHT GIVES LIGHT TO LIGHT
DISCOVER AD INFINITUM

St. Louis,
Missouri Territory
North America.

I declare that the earth is hollow, habitable within; containing a number of solid concentric spheres; one within the other, and it is open at the pole twelve or sixteen degrees. I pledge my life in support of this truth, and am ready to explore the hollow if the world will support and aid me in the undertaking.

I have ready for the press a treatise on the principles of Matter, wherein I show proofs of the above propositions, account for various phenomena, and disclose Dr. Darwin's "Golden Secret".

My terms are the patronage of this and the new world. I dedicate it to my wife and her ten children.

I select Dr. S. L. Mitchel, Sir H. Davy and Baron Alexander Von Humboldt as my protectors. I ask one hundred brave companions, well equipped, to start from Siberia, on the fall season, with reindeer and sledges, on the ice of the frozen sea; I believe we will find a warm and rich land, stocked with thrifty vegetables and animals; if not, on reaching one degree northward of latitude 82, we will return in the succeeding spring.

John Cleves Symmes of Ohio,
Late Captain of Infantry.

Predictably – although the Captain did enclose a certificate of sanity with his letter – the appeal was met with indifference virtually everywhere, Russia being the one place where it was greeted with any interest. The Czar apparently became for a time obsessed with the idea of what might be found beneath his lands, but he never translated this enthusiasm into action.

So, in an effort to drum up support at home, Symmes undertook a lecture tour of America, hoping to raise the necessary funds this way. Unfortunately

Above: Dr Edmund Halley holding a sketch of his Hollow Earth theory, from a portrait belonging to the Royal Society

Left and far left: An engraving of Captain John Symmes and of him addressing an American meeting about his Hollow Earth theories

his brusque manner with questioners did not always endear him to his audiences, although he did manage to attract one or two influential people among his supporters. One of these, Richard M. Johnson, a congressman from Kentucky who later became Vice-President of the United States, actually addressed Congress on the matter and suggested that it vote Symmes the funds to 'bring great honour and profit to America by opening up these new lands'.[6] For some reason the other senators did not share Johnson's enthusiasm, and the petition was quashed.

But Captain Symmes was not a man to be easily deterred; he published a book about his ideas, *Theory of Concentric Spheres* (1826), and continued on his whistle-stop lecture tour. But such a pace could not be kept up, and by the winter of 1828, when he had reached Canada, the strain caused him to collapse with exhaustion. Barely had he been brought back to his home town of Hamilton in Ohio, than he died aged 49. His sons erected a monument to him which still stands to this day: it reads, 'Captain John Cleves Symmes was a Philosopher, and the originator of "Symmes Theory of Concentric Spheres and Polar Voids". He contended the Earth was hollow and habitable within.'

After Symmes's death, the vogue for the Hollow Earth theory continued for a time in America, and one of the Captain's so-called supporters, a man named Joseph Reynolds, actually managed to raise enough money to launch an expedition to search for one of the entry holes. Reynolds was, however, an unscrupulous confidence trickster, and once he had obtained the necessary finance – through packing lecture halls with outlandish tales of marvellous subterranean cities guarded by twenty-foot giants – he set off amply provisioned with food and drink and was never heard of again. Some reports suggest that he got no further than the South Seas, where he settled down to a life of pleasure with native girls; others that he never even left New York, merely dropping out of sight with the money to live in comfort and obscurity for the rest of his life.

Nevertheless Symmes's theories had also caught the imagination of several writers, and two, Edgar Allan Poe and Jules Verne, were to produce classic works around his theme. Poe wrote three short stories on the idea, *MS. Found in a Bottle*, *The Unparalleled Adventure of One Hans Pfall* and *The Narrative of Arthur Gordon Pym*. Verne's work *Journey to the Centre of the Earth* is possibly the best book he ever wrote and is certainly the one publication that has done most over the years to keep the idea of a hollow earth alive.

A third literary man who took the idea still further – and whose pronouncements were to have a quite astonishing sequel fifty years later – was the English writer Lord Edward George Bulwer Lytton, author of *The Coming Race* published in 1871. This little work, now of the utmost rarity, made use of all the legends and theories about an inner world and described the life of its inhabitants. These people, the *Vril-ya*, had powers far in advance of those living on the surface, and planned in the fullness of time to emerge and conquer humanity. The book took the form of a description by a young American who accidentally stumbled on the inner world while exploring a

Top: Lord Edward Lytton, author of the controversial *The Coming Race*, and (*above*) an illustration from the 1888 edition of the book

Opposite: A dramatic moment in the film *Journey to the Centre of the Earth*

15

mine, and there learned the secret of these 'Supreme Beings' who had developed their energy, or 'vril-power' to such an extent that they were superior to anyone living on earth. A fine mixture of occult knowledge (Bulwer Lytton belonged to several English mystical societies) and storytelling, *The Coming Race* was, on its author's own admission, pure fiction.

However, fifty years later, with the emergence of Hitler and the Nazi Party in Germany, it was suddenly declared by them to be based on fact. The Fuehrer and several of the members of his High Command believed quite literally in the existence of a race of 'Super Beings' below the earth and directed extensive research to be carried out. As Dr Willy Ley, the distinguished scientist, has commented: 'So convinced were they of the actuality of Bulwer Lytton's *Vril*-race that they formed "The *Vril* Society" or "Luminous Lodge". They believed that the super race would emerge one day, and therefore set about developing their own *Vril*-power (or energy) so that they might be the equals and not the slaves of the subterraneans.'[7]

Hitler's attraction to the book is not difficult to understand: its proposal of a super race ruling the world matched his own design, just as he saw himself as the *Tur*, or dictator, of the *Vril-ya*, who considered democracy as something 'belonging to the infancy of political science.'[8]

Records discovered at the end of the war indicate that Hitler actually sent expeditions to explore German, Swiss and Italian mines to try and find the entrance Bulwer Lytton had written of yet tantalizingly refused to locate. 'As early as 1936,' the occult authority Gunther Rosenberg has written, 'the Nazis were sending teams of elite corpsmen into caves and mines in Europe. They were checking on a possible entrance into the land of *Vril-ya*. Entire crews of spelunkers prowled caves hunting for the new, advanced man.'[9]

Despite the failure of mission after mission, Hitler and his cohorts refused to be shaken in their belief. The Fuehrer even believed he had seen one of the members of the super race, as he told Hermann Rauschning, the governor of Danzig. 'The new man is living amongst us now,' he is reported to have said. 'He is here! I will tell you a secret. I have seen the new man. He is intrepid and cruel. I was afraid of him.'[10]

Were these just the ravings of a madman? Certainly the whole affair has fascinated occultists and historians ever since the end of the war: just as has the recurring legend that some senior Nazis who disappeared without trace as the Third Reich crumbled did find one of the subterranean passages and fled into the bowels of the earth.

Some time before the emergence of Hitler on the world scene another important work had appeared which first aroused real interest in the theory of polar openings, William Reed's *Phantom of the Poles* published in 1906. This book provided the first compilation of scientific evidence for the idea and was based on the reports of Arctic explorers. In it Reed estimated that the crust of the earth was 800 miles thick, while its hollow interior had a diameter of 6,400 miles. He summarized his beliefs thus: 'The earth is hollow. The Poles, so long sought, are phantoms. There are openings at the northern and

Above: Adolf Hitler, who organized searches for the entrances to the Hollow Earth

Right: A sketch of Marshall B. Gardner's concept of the inside of the earth

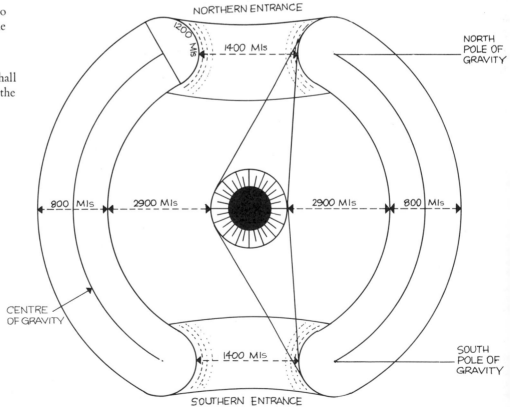

NORTHERN ENTRANCE

1200 MIs

1400 MIs

NORTH POLE OF GRAVITY

800 MIs 2900 MIs 2900 MIs 800 MIs

CENTRE OF GRAVITY

SOUTH POLE OF GRAVITY

1400 MIs

SOUTHERN ENTRANCE

southern extremities. In the interior are vast continents, oceans, mountains and rivers. Vegetable and animal life are evident in this New World, and it is probably peopled by races unknown to dwellers on the Earth's surface.'

Reed pointed out that the earth was not a true sphere, but flattened at the top and bottom, and that the poles were actually in mid-air in the centre of polar openings. It was therefore impossible for them to be discovered, and explorers thinking they had reached them had been misled by the erratic behaviour of their compasses – which, as is known, will not function within 150 miles of either of the poles.

Seven years later another somewhat similar book was privately published by an author who, as far as can be ascertained, knew nothing of William Reed's work. This was *A Journey to the Earth's Interior; or, Have the Poles Really Been Discovered?* by Marshall B. Gardner, which appeared first in 1913 and was then professionally republished in 1920 with numerous drawings and diagrams. The author maintained the book was the result of over twenty years' research.

Gardner's concept was not unlike that of Reed, but he differed in believing that there was a central sun in the hollow earth which was responsible for the magnificent display of Arctic lights known as the Aurora Borealis. He described the earth as having circular openings at the poles, approximately 1,400 miles in diameter; and the ocean water which flowed through these openings adhered to the solid crust both above and below because the centre of gravity of the earth, according to his theory, resided in the middle of this solid portion and not in its hollow interior. Because of this, said Gardner, a ship that travelled through the polar openings would continue to sail in an inverted position on the inside of the crust as it had done on the outside. He also believed that it was in the inner world that the mammoth of antiquity had originated – and indeed still lived.

Independently of each other, Reed and Gardner claimed that the temperature on the inside of the earth was more uniform than on the outside, being warmer in winter and cooler in summer. It was in fact an ideal subtropical climate, with adequate rain, no snow, and without extremes of heat and cold. Around the mouth of the polar openings, they said, was a ring of ice, the Great Massive Fresh Water Ice Pack, and it was here that icebergs originated, consisting of water that had 'flowed out from the inside of the earth'.[11]

In concluding his book, Marshall Gardner spoke of his hope for the future, which might prove the validity of his claims: 'We shall see all when we explore the Arctic in earnest, as we shall easily be able to do with the aid of airships. And when once we have seen it we shall wonder why it was for so long we were blind to evidence which, as is shown in this book, has been before men's eyes for practically a whole century and over.'

Just over thirty years later, the man Gardner had envisaged appeared in the shape of the American explorer Rear Admiral Richard E. Byrd of the United States Navy. In two expeditions, in 1947 and 1956, Byrd crossed, or entered, according to which viewpoint one accepts, the Arctic and Antarctic

Above: Marshall B. Gardner, author of *A Journey to the Earth's Interior* (1920)

Opposite: A rare photograph of Rear Admiral Byrd and (*above*) one of the extraordinary pictures of open water in the midst of ice near the North Pole

18

Poles. He apparently flew for 1,700 miles beyond the North Pole and 2,300 miles beyond the South Pole into new, unknown, iceless territories not recorded on any map, which the Hollow Earth supporters believe are the openings leading to the interior.

Reports indicate that a veil of secrecy was thrown over the Rear Admiral's mission immediately afterwards by government agencies, and only his radio messages and the contemporary newspaper reports remain as clues to what happened. Even after his death in 1957 all his personal papers were locked away.

Before Byrd left on his seven-hour North Pole flight in February 1947 he said, 'I'd like to see that land beyond the Pole. That area beyond the Pole is the centre of the Great Unknown.'[12] Some people believe that that is just what he did see, and that he must have entered the hollow earth because he could not have witnessed the iceless territory of mountains, lakes and green vegetation he reported by radio anywhere but there.

In January 1956, tackling the South Pole, the Rear Admiral sent another puzzling report. 'On January 13,' he said, 'members of the United States expedition accomplished a flight of 2,700 miles from the base at McMurdo

Sound, and penetrated a land extent of 2,300 miles beyond the Pole.'[13] Again, the Hollow Earth supporters maintained he had found 'the Great Unknown' by the other route. Byrd himself stated enigmatically on his return that 'the present expedition has opened up a vast new territory.' Ever since, there have been suggestions that the whole discovery was hushed up by the American government to prevent anyone else – the Russians in particular – seeking the territory. True or false, the episode is one of the strangest in the history of exploration.

Not long afterwards the puzzle of Rear Admiral Byrd's flights was resurrected again during the discussion of those phenomena known as Flying Saucers or Unidentified Flying Objects (UFOs). Ray Palmer, one of the world's leading experts on these mysterious objects, and the editor of *Flying Saucers* magazine, came to the conclusion that the two subjects might be related. He wrote in December 1959:

> Admiral Byrd's two flights over the Poles prove that there is a 'strangeness' about the shape of the Earth in both polar areas. Byrd flew to the North Pole but did not stop there and turn back, but went on for 1,700 miles beyond it, and then retraced his course to his Arctic base (due to his gasoline supply running low). As progress was made beyond the Pole point, iceless land and lakes, mountains covered with trees, *even a monstrous animal resembling the mammoth of antiquity* (vide Marshall B. Gardner) was seen moving through the underbush; and all this reported via radio by the plane occupants. For almost all of the 1,700 miles the plane flew over land, mountains, trees, lakes and rivers.
>
> What was this unknown land? Did Byrd, in travelling due north, enter into the hollow interior of the Earth through the north polar opening? Later Byrd's expedition went to the South Pole and after passing it, went 2,300 miles beyond it. Once again we have penetrated into an unknown and mysterious land which does not appear on today's maps. And once again we find no announcement. And, strangest of all, we find the world's millions absorbing the announcement and registering a complete blank in so far as curiosity is concerned.

Finding the evidence irrefutable that Byrd had stumbled on the two holes which led to the inner world, Palmer added his new conviction: 'The flying saucers could come from these two unknown lands "beyond the poles". It is the opinion of the editors of *Flying Saucers* magazine that the existence of these lands cannot be disproved by anyone, considering the facts of the two expeditions we have outlined . . . and that there might well be intelligences there quite capable of building and flying these craft now sighted in our heavens.'[14]

This assertion has since raised considerable support, and in 1974 one of the leading British experts on UFOs, Brinsley Le Poer Trench, published a book arguing the whole case, *Secret of the Ages: UFOs from Inside the Earth*. Mr Le Poer Trench believes that the inner world may well have been colonized originally by people from Atlantis, fleeing from the catastrophe which overwhelmed their nation, and that their advanced technology has enabled them

Above: One of the Hollow Earth features that appeared in *Amazing Stories* in May 1946, a magazine edited by Ray Palmer (*right*)

to build the flying saucers. It is with these that they have been observing us since the earliest recorded time, he says.

There has, of course, been much speculation about what the people who live inside the hollow earth might be like. A Norwegian sailor Olaf Jansen even claimed that he and his father actually sailed into the interior and met the inhabitants. 'They were giants,' he said, 'but they were friendly and we lived there for two years. There were many marvellous wonders inside the earth.'[15] Jansen reported that the interior was lit by a single sun and the very tall inhabitants possessed a mysterious power which enabled them to operate machines by drawing energy for propulsion from the air.

The giants apparently lived for at least five hundred years and were well aware of what was happening on the surface world. Jansen and his father were allowed to sail home after two years, but on the return journey the old man was killed when their boat struck an iceberg. Back in Norway the young sailor's story was mocked and derided and he never spoke about it again until, as an old man on his deathbed, he recounted his experiences to a young American journalist, Willis George Emerson. The adventure was later published as a book, *The Smoky God*, in 1908 and has remained as one more enigma in the hollow earth story.

Collectively, the underworld residents seem to be a diverse lot: different reports have described them as giants, fairies, wee people, demonic animalmen who occasionally raid the surface world for victims, and gentle, super-intelligent beings who are the survivors of Atlantis, Lemuria or a completely unknown race. The women are also said to be very beautiful, and on occasions they have made contact with the surface people – appearing as 'goddess-like women' – and producing the geniuses who have furthered man's progress and civilization.

All this fascination with the inner world idea has naturally led to a considerable amount of research in an attempt to find the underground passages which lead to it. Madame Blavatsky, the occultist and founder of the Theosophical Society, was convinced that several of these lay under Tibetan Lamaseries, as she wrote in her book *The Secret Doctrine*. Ferdinand Ossendowski in his *Beasts, Men and Gods* reported hearing tales of tunnels scattered throughout Central Asia, several of which were said to have been used by people fleeing from their enemies. Hitler, as we have read, scoured Europe for the tunnels, while even in America there are believed to be tunnels leading *somewhere* in Oregon. George Wagner, Jr wrote about these in *Search* magazine in 1967: 'One of my correspondents stated that about 75 miles northwest of Portland, Oregon, between Portland and the Seattle earth-faults, there was a city eight or ten miles underground, a coastal city with a fine harbour. It boasted more than a million inhabitants and had an excellent space port.'

There can be no denying that amongst all this speculation and conjecture there is much that is now impossible to authenticate. But just recently there has come to hand some new evidence which must certainly be the most remarkable of all – photographs taken by an American space satellite which seem to clearly indicate a hole in the North Pole: they are reproduced on these pages. The pictures were taken on 23 November 1968 by an ESSA–7 satellite and released by the Environmental Science Service Administration completely unretouched. Both show the Pole on a remarkably clear day – one of them with the area as it has always previously appeared in the million and more pictures taken by satellite, shrouded by cloud. But in the other the cloud formation has withdrawn almost completely, revealing a dark, circular area just like a hole where the pole should be. Enthusiasts have greeted this picture as a confirmation of their belief in the Hollow Earth theory; scientists are more inclined to the view that it is a vortex formation created by the spinning of the earth.

As I write, both factions are still locked in debate, each side only being able to agree that the photographs are not the result of a camera fault, nor are they mock-ups or deliberate fakes. In them, perhaps, lies a very important contribution towards solving this oldest of our mysteries.

The interior of the earth according to William Reed, an illustration that appeared in his book *The Phantom of the Poles*, published in America in 1906

A Journey into the Hollow Earth
An extract from *The Hollow Earth*
by Dr Raymond Bernard, A.B., M.A., Ph.D., New York 1969

LET US now describe a theoretical journey through the South Polar opening to the New World that lies beyond. The best air vehicle for this purpose would be a dirigible (airship), which has many advantages over the airplane. In case it ran out of fuel in this long voyage, it could radio for aid and not risk the danger of crashing to the ground.

The first stop in such an expedition heading to the South Pole would be

Tierra del Fuego at the extreme south of South America, not far from the continent of Antarctica. Here the gasoline supply could be replenished. Then the expedition would travel straight south, and after passing 90 degrees south latitude, it would proceed in the same direction, regardless of the eccentricities of the compass. In time it would leave the barren waste of Antarctic ice and enter a territory of flora and fauna, as Admiral Byrd did when he traveled past the North Pole for 1,700 miles. The expedition could then photograph the vegetable and animal life in this Land Beyond the Pole by flying low enough.

As the expedition advances into the polar opening, after the setting of the sun, there will be observed a glow in the sky which appears like a ring covering the visible horizon, formed by the aurora, which appears as long streamers of light which wave in fantastic patterns. These lights result from the reflection of the central sun on the higher strata of the atmosphere, which is illuminated for an immense area by its diverging rays. As the expedition proceeds, the auroral displays become brighter and brighter.

As the expedition advances deeper and deeper into the polar opening, the sun gets nearer and nearer to the horizon each day, and rises lower in the sky than it formerly did. It rises later and sets later. This is due to the rays being cut off by the rim of the polar aperture as the expedition enters it. Finally a strange thing happens. It is daylight when it should be night. Only it is a different daylight than we are accustomed to on the earth's surface – the sun being much dimmer and more reddish – for it is no longer the sun to which we are accustomed – the outer sun – but an inner sun which never sets and shines continually, producing perpetual daylight. Meanwhile, the temperature gets warmer and warmer, until the climate becomes tropical, a climate of perpetual summer without changes of seasons.

As the expedition proceeds, it will notice that the sun now visible is no longer moving but is stationary in the sky. Finally it will observe new strange forms of tropical plant and animal life, including prehistoric species now extinct on the surface. This will be a veritable paradise for the botanist and zoologist.

Finally the expedition will pass the polar opening and reach the hollow interior of the earth – its interior atmosphere, the native home of the flying saucers. In time the expedition will commence to see signs of civilization and the subterranean cities of the Atlanteans and Lemurians who colonized this world many thousands of years ago, the creators of the flying saucers. The members of the expedition will then land and contact these highly civilized people who will have much to teach them that will be of utmost value to the human race. The message that they will deliver will probably relate to saving humanity from nuclear annihilation. Perhaps these people hope to prevent the coming of World War III in the near future. Or perhaps they are concerned with saving a remnant of the human race in the event that the rest of humanity is exterminated, and colonizing them in their Subterranean World, so that the human race might not be entirely destroyed. These Atlanteans should have much sympathy for us because their civilization also was destroyed by a nuclear war followed by a flood, from which they saved themselves in time by finding refuge in the Subterranean World. Since they foresee the same danger to us, they would probably like to save us in the same way they saved themselves when the rest of their countrymen perished.

Therefore, the members of this expedition may accomplish a mission of the utmost importance to the human race and may be hailed in the future not merely as the greatest explorers in history but as true Nuclear Age Saviours.

II
LOST
WORLDS

Eighteenth-century engraving of the inhabitants and monuments of Easter Island from *Charts and Plates to La Pérouse's Voyage*

Above: The location of the 'Lost World' of Roraima – a sketch from the *Observer*, October 1973

T HE IDEA of the Lost World, the community of men and women cut off from the rest of civilization, is an enduring and popular ancient mystery. Throughout the world there are to be found traditions and stories of groups of people who have, either because of the nature of their location or through deliberate choice, remained apart from the rest of us. With the passage of time and the growing advances in exploration techniques, many of these tales have been revealed for what they are, just tales, while others have proved to have some element of truth in them, though mostly nothing like the glamour of the legend.

Perhaps the most famous Lost World story among the English-speaking peoples is that which was immortalized by Sir Arthur Conan Doyle in his novel *The Lost World* (1912) based on the legends surrounding the vast plateau of Roraima, which rises to 9,000 feet and lies across the borders of Guyana, Venezuela and Brazil in South America. Conan Doyle's marvellously evocative story described the adventures of a band of explorers led by the rumbustious but resourceful Professor Challenger which succeeded in scaling the plateau and there found still alive creatures from the Stone Age – 'great flesh-eating dinosaurs', 'iguanadons, the great three-toed leaf-eater' and, most dramatically of all, 'ape men with long arms and enormous chests'.

Despite being avowedly a piece of fiction, *The Lost World* was firmly based on fact, and when Doyle wrote of the danger explorers faced he knew all about the local vampire bat which transmits paralytic rabies and sucks the blood of humans and cattle at dawn or dusk without its victims being aware of the fact; also the deadly snakes which could crush a jaguar to death and penetrate a leather shoe with their bite, and the variety of highly poisonous spiders and scorpions. He knew, too, that the rivers of the region were rich in alluvial diamonds and had his successful band of explorers return with gems to the value of £200,000.

In September 1973 a party of British climbers finally set out to discover the truth about the 'Lost World'. They were led by Don Whillans, the Everest veteran, Joe Brown, then Britain's best known rock climber, Mo Anthoine and Adrian Thompson, a tropical vegetation expert with special knowledge of the area. The climb up the sheer 2,000-foot escarpment on the Guyana side leading to the plateau proved arduous in the extreme, and was made more difficult by the huge rock fissures, some of which were believed to be 1,000 feet deep, and the hordes of deadly insects lying in wait in the crevices. During this climb the odds against their solving the age-old mystery seemed to grow longer as the party began to suffer first from injuries, food shortage and difficulties with the porters, and then from near disasters on the rock face as they approached the top. On one occasion Hamish MacInnes, the chronicler of the party, wrote, 'The main aim of the expedition hangs in the balance. We are tired, and Roraima is certainly a tough nut to crack.'[16]

At this point a storm prevented any further progress for three days, but the enforced rest gave the men renewed energy, and when they began climbing again it was with new heart. Then, at 1.30 a.m. on Sunday 10 November the main assault party of Whillans, Anthoine and MacInnes finally broke through and set foot upon the 'Lost World'. Were the legends true? Was it a world where time had stood still? Hamish MacInnes wrote later: 'The Plateau is flat – solid rock in weird formations – with mushroom-shaped knolls and saucer-like depressions, full of exotic plants. It was like arriving in heaven

Above: 'A Distant View of the Plateau', an illustration from the 1912 edition of *The Lost World* by Sir Arthur Conan Doyle, and (*right*) the real thing – the plateau of Roraima photographed by Hamish MacInnes in 1974

after a climb from hell. We fired a rocket from the summit, and wandered as if in a dream. We found that the summit was bounded by crevasses too deep and wide to be crossed except with ladders, and it was clear that the map-makers had guessed inaccurately at the configuration of this unexplored territory.'

But what about the strange creatures and men from the dawn of time, the world wanted to know? Was there any truth in Doyle's novel and the old stories?

MacInnes went on, 'We can report that there were no pterodactyls or iguanodons, but the "nasties" – scorpions, spiders and snakes – combined with exceptional climbing hazards to almost defeat us. We did, though, discover a new variety of spider, and but for the torrential rain that began to fall and finally drove us back down again, we might well have found other things.'[17]

Another famous novel which focused interest on an unexplained mystery was H. Rider Haggard's *King Solomon's Mines*, published in 1895 and still avidly read to this day. The book drew on the legend of one of the strangest archaeological sites in Africa, the ruins known as Zimbabwe in north-east Rhodesia. Haggard wrote the story at a time when much debate was going on about the origins of the site, which lies about seventeen miles south-east of Fort Victoria and a few miles from the main road linking Salisbury to Johannesburg in South Africa. One point of view had it that the ruins were the handiwork of some long lost African civilization, while its opponents felt that the construction was far too ambitious to have been the work of black natives and must have been built by Arab or Asian visitors. Rider Haggard simply took the old legend that King Solomon had once created mines full of jewels and precious metals somewhere in Africa, and to this wedded Zimbabwe – not forgetting the intrepid Allan Quartermain who, having found the mines, only narrowly escaped with his life when trapped in them by an African sorceress.

Although legends of King Solomon's Mines had existed since Roman times (the Emperor Nero, for instance, actually sent an expedition of legionaries to Africa to search for them), the stories were only taken to have some factual origin when explorers began to press into the interior of Africa, the 'Dark Continent', opening up whole new regions there in the middle of the nineteenth century. While the other major continents of the world, Asia, America and Australia, had already been penetrated by intrepid explorers, the heart of Africa was still unknown and men set out with their minds full of stories of great cities of gold, ruins full of ancient treasures, and not a soul to stop them helping themselves.

The first European to set eyes on Zimbabwe appears to have been a German geologist, Karl Mauch, who was given to wandering, on his own and on foot, through the interior of the country. He came across the array of ruins in 1872, partly through the help of a German–American ivory hunter known as Adam Renders who had heard of the ruins before but dismissed them until Mauch told him of their importance, and partly through the guidance of

Top: The 'route to King Solomon's Mines' from a 1902 edition of the famous novel by Rider Haggard (*above*). *Opposite:* A Walter Paget illustration from the same book

Above: A plan of the site of Zimbabwe from G. Caton-Thompson's *The Zimbabwe Culture*, published in 1931

Above right: The Acropolis at Zimbabwe

Below left: The famous Conical Tower in the elliptical building, which is situated on the plain beneath the Acropolis

Below right: An aerial view of the elliptical building

local natives. Although the ruins were overgrown with vegetation, Mauch could distinguish various different constructions among them and was convinced that the building on the hillside was an imitation of King Solomon's temple in Mount Moriah while the large rounded structure in the valley was a copy of the palace in which the Queen of Sheba had stayed when she visited Solomon.

The discovery, once it was announced to the world, soon conjured up visions of gold and precious jewels, and fortune hunters of all kinds flocked to the district. By 1900 there were 114,000 gold claims registered in the surrounding countryside, most beside ancient workings, and the desecration of history went on quite wantonly. 'The damage done', J. D. Schofield later reported, 'was immense, for everything except the gold was treated in a most reckless manner.'[18]

Against this background of destruction the first geologists tried to ascertain the date and purpose of Zimbabwe and its buildings, clearing and restoring the quarter-of-a-square-mile site as best they could after the ravages of the fortune hunters – whose numbers had included one particularly unscrupulous crowd with the high-sounding title of 'The Ancient Ruins Company' who certainly left in ruins every site they touched! In examining the location, the experts were struck by the largeness of the overall concept, its lonely dignity and strength, and the skilful way in which the tall, girdling walls, the towers and the rounded gateways had been built. Two of the buildings stood out from the rest; the first, a strong, defensive structure, was placed on a 90-foot precipice and became known as the 'Acropolis', while the second, an elliptical building, 300 feet long by 220 feet wide, was sited on the plain beneath and was named the 'temple'. The remaining dozen ruins spread north and east of the elliptical building. All were made of local granite, of flat, brick-like stones chopped skilfully from wide 'leaves' of naturally split granite rock, and laid without any form of bonding. Having studied the ruins, Basil Davidson tells us in *Old Africa Rediscovered* (1961), two schools of thought emerged about the creators – the 'Phoenician' and 'Medieval':

> Zimbabwe, thought the first school, had a "minimum age of three milleniums": there were two main periods of building, the earlier being Sabaean of from 2000 to 1000 BC, and the later being Phoenician "somewhat anterior to 1100 BC down to some time before the Christian era". This school of thought reflected the King Solomon's Mines' pioneers and was resolutely sure that no "natives" had ever taken a hand in this building of a civilisation. It evolved many variations; and there is scarcely a people of high antiquity whose influence was thought to have been absent here at one time or another.
>
> The second school of thought – the archaeological and scientific school – first made itself heard through David Randall-MacIver, an Egyptologist who examined the stone ruins of Southern Rhodesia in 1905 on behalf of the British Association. He concluded that those at Great Zimbabwe and others of their kind were African in origin and medieval or post-medieval in date, basing this on an investigation of seven from which no object, as he said, had been obtained by himself or others "which can be shown to be more ancient than the fourteenth or fifteenth centuries".

31

Right: The lush Pacific island of Ponape and (*far right*) a new sketch map of the remarkable ruins of Metalanim

Below: A stone gateway which stands amongst the Nan Matol ruins

The two viewpoints became the centre of heated controversy in the years which followed, and did not abate until 1929 when the British Association sent a second expedition, led by the skilled archaeologist Dr Gertrude Caton-Thompson, to try and resolve the matter. In her fascinating and exhaustive survey *The Zimbabwe Report* (1931) she came down firmly on the side of the second school and concluded, 'Examination of all the existing evidence gathered from every quarter still can produce not one single item that is not in accordance with the claim of Bantu origin and medieval date.'

Even so, the ultra-rationalist Dr Caton-Thompson could not deny that the magnificence and strangeness of the ruins still left a question mark over them. She wrote in her book, 'Zimbabwe is a mystery which lies in the still pulsating heart of native Africa' – and so it has remained. We may well never know who really built the settlement, and certainly few years are going to pass without further theories and ideas being put forward. Perhaps the most intriguing of recent years was that advanced by the Bantu witchdoctor Wuzamazulu Mutwa, who claimed in his book *Indaba, My Children* (1968) that black Africans were descended from a race of people who were once red and knew all about space travel, robots and radioactivity. And, said the witchdoctor, it was the early descendants of these people who actually built the fortress in Southern Rhodesia, calling it Zima-mbje.

A third mystery site which has become immortalized in fiction is the ruins of Nan Matol at Ponape, one of the American Caroline Islands, in the Pacific Ocean. It is probably best known as the basis for Abraham Merritt's outstand-

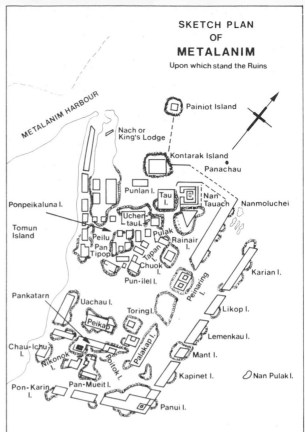

SKETCH PLAN
OF
METALANIM
Upon which stand the Ruins

METALANIM HARBOUR

Painiot Island

Nach or King's Lodge

Kontarak Island
Panachau

Punlan I.

Tau I.

Nan Tauach

Nanmoluchei

Ponpeikaluna I.

Uchen tauL

Tomun Island

Peilu

Pulak

Rainair I.

Pan Tipop

Japan

Chuok I.

Karian I.

Pun-ilel I.

Peinaring I.

Pankatarn

Uachau I.

Toring I.

Likop I.

Peikap

Lemenkau I.

Chau-Ichu I.

Nikonok

Poitok I.

Palakap I.

Mant I.

Pon-Karin I.

Pan-Mueit I.

Kapinet I.

Nan Pulak I.

Panui I.

ing novels, *The Moon Pool* and *The Conquest of the Moon Pool* (both 1919), but Edgar Rice Burroughs, the creator of Tarzan, and Talbot Mundy have similarly utilized the legend. Since its discovery it has been variously claimed to be the remains of a lost continent, the capital of a once-great Pacific empire, or – more prosaically – the fortress of Spanish pirates.

The island of Ponape, sitting almost on the equator, is the largest of the Carolines, and in one of its bays, called Tomun, stands a vast array of what look like square islets made of dark blue stone – the natives know them as Nan Matol. The ruins, which cover an area of eleven square miles, tower up to as much as thirty feet high, and when the tide is full the area is said to resemble 'a deserted Venice of the Pacific'.[19] Examination of the ruins has shown that the 'blue stone' of which they are made is prismatic basalt – of the same type as the Giant's Causeway in Ireland – and that it was originally obtained from the island of Jokaz, some fifteen miles away on the northern coast of Ponape.

In his description of the island in *Ancient Ruins and Archaeology* (1964), L. Sprague de Camp writes: 'Nan Matol is an awesome ruin in spite of damage from hurricanes, treasure hunters and the prying action of tropical vegetation. Most of the islets are bounded by enormous walls . . . which are built of long columnar pieces of dark rock laid crisscross, like the logs of a log cabin, and rivetted on the inner sides by masses of coral piled up against them. Several canals, swarming with sharks and rays, lap at these walls even at lower tide.'

It is doubtful whether the first sailors who made landfalls on Ponape during the sixteenth century saw Nan Matol, because of its isolated situation; indeed even today it is only possible to reach the ruins by means of a fifteen-mile motorboat ride. The first detailed description of the site does not appear to have been written until 1853 when a shipwrecked Irishman, James O'Connell, who had made his home on Ponape and married the chief's daughter, recorded his adventures in a book. O'Connell was clearly overwhelmed by the ruins, which he said were sited in a kingdom known to the natives as Metalanim. 'But the most wonderful adventure during one excursion,' he wrote, 'the relation of which will put my credit to a severer test than any other fact detailed, was the discovery of a large uninhabited island, upon which were the most stupendous ruins of a character of architecture differing altogether from the present style of the islanders, and of an extent truly astonishing.'[20] O'Connell appears to have had the utmost difficulty in exploring the ruins or finding anything out about their origins because they were believed to be the residence of evil spirits and therefore avoided by the natives. Nonetheless, his account did attract the attention of others, and a succession of investigators have subsequently studied the ruins in the hope of piercing their mystery.

Folklore maintained that Nan Matol was the handiwork of two young wizards who cast a spell which caused the blue stone to be transported to the bay and there erected as a great cult centre for the worship of the gods. A more rational explanation was that the site had been built by a long forgotten conqueror of Ponape (the Carolines have no written traditions) as the centre of his island empire. Of this, Sprague de Camp has written, 'Once Nan Matol was made up of several different groups of structures. The main centre is Matol-Pa, the lower city, where dwelt the king. The upper city, Matol-Pau-Ue, includes the tallest building in Nan Matol, Nan Towas, "the Place of the High Walls" where the kings were buried and Es-En-Tau, the house of the high priests. The third section consists mainly of sea walls, canal borders, and other retaining walls. Near the south end of the ruins is Pan Katera, the sacred governmental centre including a palace and altars for offerings.' In addition, a German scientist Dr Paul Hambruch was told in 1910 that the site had once been the centre of worship of a turtle god, Nanusunsap, which had apparently ceased under mysterious circumstances in about 1800.

Several occult groups, including the Theosophists, have claimed that Nan Matol is a relic of Lemuria, one of the great sunken continents of legend which we shall be considering later in the book. In his unashamedly fictional work *The Moon Pool* Abraham Merritt presented the ruins as being the entrance to an underground world where a civil war is being waged by a strange advanced civilization. Unfortunately for both these views, there seems no reason to believe that the building of Nan Matol was in any way the work of an advanced culture. So the mystery of the sea-swept ruins remains, with the likelihood that if its real meaning is ever established it will have some connection with religious worship: probably involving a deity and cult long since departed from human remembrance.

Another ancient mystery in the Pacific which has also been associated with the 'lost world' of Lemuria is Easter Island, one of the loneliest spots on earth, and the site of a weird array of over 600 giant stone heads which stand, backs to the ocean, gazing across the hills and valleys of the land. Easter Island, which is over a thousand miles from its nearest neighbour Pitcairn Island and two thousand from the coast of South America, is said by occultists to be yet another visible sign of the great empire of Lemuria which once spread right across the Pacific: but what even they cannot offer is an explanation of the meaning of the heads.

A close-up of the dramatic features of the Easter Island statues

Above: Australian aborigines dance the myth of creation at the circumcision ceremony of the tribe's boys and (*left*) an aborigine made up for such a ceremony

Opposite above: An aborigine witch-doctor

Opposite below: Two of the strange cave paintings in the Kimberley Ranges which some have suggested might represent spacemen who once visited Australia

Indeed all attempts at deciphering these stone wonders since they were first recorded by the Dutch admiral Jacob Roggeveen when he landed on Easter Sunday, 1722, have only served to heighten the mystery. The number of heads still to be seen is believed to be far smaller than the original total; some have fallen into the sea, others have been destroyed, the remainder stolen. The sculptures, for such they obviously are, range in size from a mere three feet to thirty-six feet in height; some, which were never erected, measure an enormous sixty-six feet in length and lie on the ground surrounded by the tools which were used to make them: of the workers who seemingly so carelessly abandoned their task there is no trace. Excavation around the bases of the heads has shown that, below ground, they have small squat bodies, but whether these were ever intended to be visible is hard to say.

What has intrigued scientists almost as much as the statues themselves is the question of how the Easter Islanders came to such an isolated place; the voyages of Thor Heyerdahl and his theories concerning mass migration have aroused much interest in this context. Heyerdahl, like many others, was puzzled by the light-skinned features of the people, which seemed to indicate an origin many thousands of miles away. But how had they travelled such a huge distance and evolved the skills necessary for producing the huge statues? As a result of study and practical experiment he came to the conclusion that the islanders might be the product of an intermingling of the Nordic, Peruvian and Polynesian cultures, and that they had found their way to the island on raft boats. Once there, he believed, they were unable to repair or rebuild any of their craft because of the lack of vegetation on the island, and therefore, being unable to go on, settled down to make the best of things. Initially, they put their skill to work on projects such as the giant heads, but with the passing of time and the debilitating effects of isolation they fell into indolence, and by the time the Europeans arrived even folk memories about the creation of the statues had gone.[21] Such is one theory: another affirms the heads to be merely representations of the people of Lemuria (who were giants), while a third says they are the handiwork of visitors from another world. As far as the islanders themselves are concerned, the statues exist and that is all that matters: others may puzzle for as long as they wish to try and find a meaning!

Perhaps, though, the strangest of all Lost World stories is that concerning Australia – to most people simply the newest of continents, but to scientists and geographers an enigma, and just possibly the homeland of all mankind. For much of its history the country was completely unknown to the rest of the world, even its nearest neighbours, and while rumours and legends of most great nations existed long before they were actually found (for example, America), Australia appeared almost literally out of the blue to the Dutch Captain Jansz in 1606.

Yet, as experts have pointed out, geologically it is the oldest continent in the world, for in the north-west is a shield of land that has probably been above water for 1,600 million years. It is the oldest in human terms too, because its only inhabitants before 1788 were Stone Age people, members of

The extraordinary formation in the Northern Territory of Australia known by aborigines as the 'Many-Headed Mountain', otherwise known as the Olgas

the only known race which could have served as a common ancestor for all mankind. Some of these people, it is said, may have been living in Tasmania in the Ice Age 30,000 years ago.

Australia has proved baffling in the extreme, for where other great countries have provided endless ruins, artifacts, traditions both oral and recorded, even people, for study by experts, here there was virtually nothing: only a continent of vast, empty spaces, a few strange-looking animals and 300,000 nomadic Aborigines spread so thinly that even they must have seemed almost non-existent. As one commentator, Charles Berlitz, has put it, 'The aspect to the first explorers must have seemed like some lunar landscape.'[22]

With the passage of time, it has been possible to gain a certain insight into the early days of this strange place through study of the Aborigine legends, as Louis Pauwels and Jacques Bergier report in *The Eternal Man* (1972):

The myths of Australia relate that the earth gradually emerged from a primordial sea. They all begin with the 'ages of the dream', eternally present and the sources of all life, the reign of the heroic celestial creators, fathers of shamanism, who lived in heaven in a place which was filled with cool water and quartz crystals. These were the gods who ruled over procreation and death, both of which were supernatural. Another hero, sometimes wise, sometimes foolish, was the mediator between gods and men. He transmitted the rudiments of knowledge, technology and magic medicine. Running through all these myths there seems to be a taboo on change and evasion as if the endless expanses of Australia were really a sort of penal colony for these first men.

The idea that the continent might have been a 'penal colony' long before the arrival of the British is one that has intrigued those of a speculative mind. Scientists are agreed that Australia probably enjoyed a much milder climate towards the end of the Pleistocene Age, and the question now is: did a race of men once live here whose contemporaries the Aborigines were for a time, or even whose last remnants they are?

Because of a lack of ruins and other appropriate sites, excavations in Australia have been on a fairly limited scale, but not without success. In 1929 a number of primitive implements were discovered in the valley of the Murray River near Adelaide which carbon testing showed to date from about 3000 BC. More spectacular finds were made between 1960 and 1964 when 850 stone items were dug up at Keniff Cave in South Queensland and carbon-dated as being at least 16,000 years old. Then in 1965 a well-preserved skeleton was found in a gravel quarry at Keilor near Melbourne – an astonishing discovery – and dating shows it to be 16,000 years old, too. But who might have left these remains? Let Pauwels and Bergier speculate for us once again:

> Today we can imagine that the unknown men came in masses when the climate was most favourable when there were broad, flowing rivers, when lakes full of fish were surrounded by luxuriant vegetation and when gigantic herbivorous marsupials supplied the immigrants with food, but dangerous beasts of prey were non-existent. By what sea-route did this immigration take place? For what reason? Was it the exodus of a whole race? The formation of a "reserve" on a continent with no hidden dangers? Fear of some peril to which mankind was exposed? Was it an experiment performed by superior beings? Did they choose this gigantic, uninhabited territory to deposit their knowledge in? Were enormous masses of workers brought there to bury this knowledge? Worker commandos in the dream sands of kangaroo land!

The idea of 'superior beings' has cropped up in connection with the strange paintings found in 1838 in a cave near Glenelg River in the Kimberley Ranges in Western Australia. One of the paintings shows a group of four figures, all with haloes of dark blue and wearing sandals on their feet. The idea of people wearing shoes when all Aborigines went barefoot set the first puzzle; the second was the fact that the figures had variously three or seven fingers and toes. According to archaeologists, the paintings were the work of Aborigines and represented their rain god Wandjina. The Aborigines, for their part, denied this stoutly, as the investigator Andrew Tomas wrote in a report in 1972: 'The Aborigines say they were made by another race. The technique of art-work and the employment of a blue pigment not used by the Aborigines, attributes the authorship of these drawings to a people of non-Australian origin. These "Wandjina" pictures are supposed to represent the first men.'[23]

It has recently been suggested that these figures are actually spacemen who visited Australia in primitive times. The same explanation has also been offered for another still more striking painting found in the same caves. This lone figure, ten feet tall, is wearing a long, sack-like pink garment, and surrounding

Above: This monolith which looks like the keep of an ancient castle is Mount Conner, Northern Territory

Below: Another Northern Territory phenomenon, Ayers Rock, which changes colour during the day

his head, like a helmet, are two circles of pink and gold. On the pink band are six strange symbols which it has so far proved impossible to interpret. Again the major arguments centre on whether this is the work of Aborigine or immigrant hands.

Apart from men from other worlds visiting ancient Australia, there is some controversial evidence that both the Egyptians and the Chinese may have landed on the continent in the dim past. At Darwin a hard stone figure of the Chinese deity Shou Lao was found during excavations, but whether it is just an isolated relic or the first clue to an actual Chinese settlement only further work will show. In 1963 a pile of Egyptian coins that had been buried about 4,000 years ago was found in some rocky terrain in an undisclosed location. Indeed the find was barely publicized at all, and photographs of the coins only appeared in a few obscure publications. The very enormity of the idea of any kind of contact between Ancient Egypt and Australia seems to have discouraged speculation.

Perhaps if any answers to the puzzle of a lost world in Australia are going to be found they will emerge in the heart of the Australian desert at Lyndavale, where this vast, sandy plain is suddenly broken by three extraordinary masses aligned in an east-west direction over a distance of about eighty miles. Robert Charroux describes these monoliths in *The Mysterious Unknown* (1969): 'The first, Mount Conner, is of quartzite, and looks like the keep of a mediaeval castle. The second is a rounded granite hummock, known as Ayers Rock, and is considered by Australians to be one of the marvels of the mineral world. The third, of sandstone and granite, forms a circlet of minarets, domes and

pillars, which the aborigines name the Many-Headed Mountain. These monoliths lie in an absolute straight line, so that an observer standing in line with the first or last cannot see the other two.'

Geologists who have examined these strange creations believe they are of natural origin, just freaks of erosion. The Aborigines, however, say they originated from the 'Dream Time' and were actually carved by the Arientas and Luritchas, half-man and half-animal creatures. Today, say these enigmatic oldest residents of the great continent, the monoliths stand as a memorial to mankind's predecessors. . . .

Sir Arthur Conan Doyle

Discovering the Lost World
An extract from *The Lost World* by Sir Arthur Conan Doyle, London 1912

"AFTER MANY adventures which I need not describe, and after travelling a distance which I will not mention, in a direction which I withhold, we came at last to a tract of country which has never been described, nor, indeed, visited save by one unfortunate predecessor. Would you kindly look at this?"

Professor Challenger handed me a photograph – half-plate size.

"The unsatisfactory appearance of it is due to the fact," said he, "that on descending the river the boat was upset and the case which contained the undeveloped films was broken, with disastrous results. Nearly all of them were totally ruined – an irreparable loss. This is one of the few which partially escaped. This explanation of deficiencies or abnormalities you will kindly accept. There was talk of faking. I am not in a mood to argue such a point."

The photograph was certainly very off-coloured. An unkind critic might easily have misinterpreted that dim surface. It was a dull grey landscape, and as I gradually deciphered the details of it I realized that it represented a long and enormously high line of cliffs exactly like an immense cataract seen in the distance, with a sloping, tree-clad plain in the foreground.

"I believe it is the same place as the painted picture," said I.

"It *is* the same place," the Professor answered. "I found traces of the fellow's camp. Now look at this."

It was a nearer view of the same scene, though the photograph was extremely defective. I could distinctly see the isolated, tree-crowned pinnacle of rock which was detached from the crag.

"I have no doubt of it at all," said I.

"Well, that is something gained," said he. "We progress, do we not? Now, will you please look at the top of that rocky pinnacle? Do you observe something there?"

"An enormous tree."

"But on the tree?"

"A large bird," said I.

He handed me a lens.

"Yes," I said, peering through it, "a large bird stands on the tree. It appears to have a considerable beak. I should say it was a pelican."

"I cannot congratulate you upon your eyesight," said the Professor. "It is not a pelican nor indeed is it a bird. It may interest you to know that I succeeded in shooting that particular specimen. It was the only absolute proof of my experiences which I was able to bring away with me."

"You have it then?" Here at last was tangible corroboration.

"I had it. It was unfortunately lost with so much else in the same boat accident which ruined my photographs. I clutched at it as it disappeared in the swirl of the rapids and part of its wing was left in my hand. I was insensible when washed ashore but the miserable remnant of my superb specimen was still intact; I now lay it before you."

From a drawer he produced what seemed to me to be the upper portion of the wing of a large bat. It was at least two feet in length, a curved bone, with a membranous veil beneath it.

"A monstrous bat!" I suggested.

"Nothing of the sort," said the Professor, severely. "Living, as I do, in an educated and scientific atmosphere, I could not have conceived that the first principles of zoology were so little known. Is it possible that you do not know the elementary fact in comparative anatomy, that the wing of a bird is really the forearm, while the wing of a bat consists of three elongated fingers with membranes between? Now, in this case, the bone is certainly not the forearm, and you can see for yourself that this is a single membrane hanging upon a single bone, and therefore that it cannot belong to a bat. But if it is neither bird nor bat, what is it?"

My small stock of knowledge was exhausted.

"I really do not know," said I.

He opened the standard work to which he had already referred me.

"Here," said he, pointing to the picture of an extraordinary flying monster, "is an excellent reproduction of the dimorphodon, or pterodactyl, a flying reptile of the Jurassic period. On the next page is a diagram of the mechanism of its wing. Kindly compare it with the specimen in your hand."

A wave of amazement passed over me as I looked. I was convinced. There could be no getting away from it. The cumulative proof was overwhelming. The sketch, the photographs, the narrative, and now the actual specimen – the evidence was complete. I said so – I said so warmly, for I felt that the Professor was an ill-used man. He leaned back in his chair with drooping eyelids and a tolerant smile, basking in this sudden gleam of sunshine.

"It's just the very biggest thing that I ever heard of!" said I, though it was my journalistic rather than my scientific enthusiasm that was roused. "It is colossal. You are a Columbus of science who has discovered a lost world. I'm really awfully sorry if I seemed to doubt you. It was all so unthinkable. But I understand evidence when I see it, and this should be good enough for anyone."

INDIA superior

Cathay

Quinsai

NO   VVS

Terra florida

Archipelagus 7448
Insularu

Zipangri

Chamaho

Panuco Inf. Tortucaru

CVBA

Iucatana

Hispaniola

Temistiran

Cozumela

S. P. E.

Iamica

Beragna

nf. pdonum

P A R I A falb
auro & marg

ORBIS

Catigara

Insula Atlatica quam uocant
& Americam

Inf. infortu
natæ

Regió G

Calensuan

Mare pacificum

Fretu

On the map:

ISCA

C. Britónum

Cortereal

Exteriores

Hispan

Oceanus occidentalis

Medera

Fortunatæ inf.

Inf. Hefperidum

APRICA pars

Antilla

Dominica

S. Iacobi

Sinus Atlanticus

Canibali

7. infule Mar guentarū

Munster's famous map of North and South America, 1540

THE YEAR 1492 is one of the few in history that remain indelibly printed on the mind of even the most indifferent scholar – the year when Christopher Columbus set foot in the new world and thereby 'discovered' America. Although the greatness of Columbus's achievement has never been seriously questioned, there seems little doubt that he was far from being the first explorer to reach the continent: indeed voyagers may well have stood on the eastern shores of the Americas as many as a thousand years before the Spanish party.

Modern research into historical records has in fact shown that there were tales of a 'land to the west' in many ancient cultures, a good number of them dating hundreds and even thousands of years before the voyage of Columbus. This quest by man for new horizons beyond the sunset seems to have influenced great philosophers just as much as great explorers and inspired myths and legends for centuries. Hence we can find claims of differing validity for discovering America among the Greeks, Romans, English, Scottish, Welsh, Irish, French, Spanish, Dutch and Portuguese, not to mention other such seafaring folk as the Chinese, Japanese, Egyptians, Phoenicians, Hebrews, Arabs, and Turks. All certainly had ships quite capable of crossing the Atlantic (or, in the case of the Oriental nations, the Pacific) on even the most erratic courses. The major claims are examined here: the rest are of a much more intangible nature and await the student in other more scholarly works than this popular history.

Aside from the explorers, it has been established by carbon dating that there was human habitation in America at least 12,000 years ago. Some legends even have it that the continent was populated much earlier than this, indeed that man actually originated in America: but attempts to substantiate such claims have always failed.

Although it may prove a source of chagrin to some modern Americans, it seems highly likely that the first outsiders to reach America were Mongoloid inhabitants of eastern Russia, who came not by sea but across the Bering Straits, when there was still a land bridge between the two great continents, somewhere between 20,000 and 40,000 years ago. They travelled down the Pacific coast and on into Central and South America – as the physical characteristics of the American Indian suggest. To support this theory, stone implements have been found in both America and Siberia which show every indication of being the handiwork of the same culture.

This boat, modelled on that in which St Brendan is said to have sailed to America in the sixth century, is being used by a modern expedition to retrace the saint's route

The Chinese, too, are said to have reached the continent by way of the Northern Pacific as early as the fifth century AD. The Chinese civilization is, as we know, one of the oldest in the world and its records are among the fullest and most reliable. It was as a result of years of study of such documents and maps that the theory of the Chinese discovery of America in AD 458 was advanced a few years ago by the distinguished Peking professor Chu Shien-chi. He says the discovery was made by a Buddhist priest named Hoei Shin who sailed across the Pacific with four other monks and made a landfall in Mexico, or at least somewhere on the coast of Central America, which he named Fusang, after a Chinese plant which rather resembled some vegetation he found growing in the new country. A number of students are of the opinion that the whole story is invented because of the rather incredible adventures related in Hoei Shin's narrative (he claims, in one instance, that there was a land peopled entirely by women not far from Fusang), but others have pointed out that sculptures have been unearthed in the ruins of Central American cities which are identical with those used in the Buddhist religion. Although the Chinese are fully convinced of the validity of their claim – Hoei Shin's voyage now being an established fact in Chinese history – the story obviously requires much more investigation.

More widespread credibility is probably given to the first European claimant, an Irish saint named Brendan who lived between about 484 and 577. St Brendan, who came from Killarney, was an experienced seaman and navigator, and made his voyage in a thirty-six-foot-long wooden-framed boat, covered with ox-hides greased with butter to make the craft waterproof. The story of the adventure is recounted in the anonymous tenth-century Latin work, the *Navigatio Sancti Brendani*, and tells how Brendan and fourteen monks set out to find the 'Promised Land'. They first sailed to the 'islands of sheep and birds' (possibly two of the Faroe Islands), then traversed 'a hellish region of fire and brimstone' (the volcanoes of Iceland?), sighted a 'floating block of crystal' (certainly an iceberg) and then went through 'an area of dense mist' (the Newfoundland Banks?) before making their landfall in 'a country of autumn sunshine, well-wooded, with a great river', which experts think could have been Labrador. Other parts of the narrative are more difficult to translate into real terms, and certainly scholars have long been puzzled by the story that Brendan landed on a whale which helped him and his crew on their way, and that angels disguised as birds also lent a hand from time to time.

Although it is hoped shortly to put the likelihood of this voyage to the test by retracing it in a boat of similar construction, there is little doubt that the Irish made numerous long-distance voyages at this time. Archaeologists have found wrecks of skin boats and habitations in Greenland dating from before the arrival of the Vikings, and, according to the Sagas, a colony of Irish monks on Iceland fled westward from the approaching Norsemen in a fleet of curraghs, leaving behind their bells, books and croziers.

The Vikings are, of course, the most famous figures in the story of the search for America before Columbus. The ancient sagas of these people – like those of *The Greenlanders*, *Eirik the Red* (father of Leif Eiriksson) and the *Eyrbyggja* – are full of tales of exploration and great heroism as men set out to find the land beyond the sea, variously referred to as 'Markland', 'Helluland' and 'Vinland the Good'. Their explorations have, in fact, come in for as much study and research as those of Columbus himself, and a welter of books have both argued for their success and conjectured as to what they found and where they went. Much of the study has focused around two topics: the voyages of the great Leif Eiriksson and the fiercely debated Vinland Map.

Eiriksson was a skilled mariner who sailed beyond the normal Viking routes to Greenland and around the year 1000 reached the coast of North America, at what is now Newfoundland. He carried some of the first settlers to this 'New World' and became the inspiration for later similar trips. It was in this 'Vinland' that Leif built his 'big houses' as he called them and thereby created the first settlement on the continent. Modern research by several scholars, including the redoubtable Norwegian Dr Helge Ingstad, has now established that this colony was located on the northern tip of Newfoundland at a place called L'Anse aux Meadows. It was here, after a fruitless search for relics along much of the coast of North America, that Dr Ingstad and others located the actual stone foundations of eight houses, a smithy, four boat sheds and two cooking pits, plus implements, all of which have been carbon-dated to the Viking era, thereby authenticating the settlement beyond any doubt. 'The site', Dr Ingstad has said, 'furnishes the first incontrovertible archaeological proof that Europeans set foot in America centuries before 1492.'[24]

It has been suggested by some scholars that the Newport Tower, a small

Above and opposite above: Two illustrations from *The Rulers of the Sea* by Edmond Neukomm, published in America in 1896, showing Vikings sighting America and exploring the continent.

Right: A photograph, taken from the same book, of the statue of Leif Eiriksson in Norway

Far right: The Newport Tower on Rhode Island which is thought may be the handiwork of Vikings

stone structure which stands in the centre of Newport on Rhode Island, is the handiwork of Vikings who followed the lead of Eiriksson in exploring America. The construction is circular in shape, about twenty-four feet high, and is said to have been a church of some type built in the eleventh or twelfth century. Opponents of the Viking theory believe it to be of a later date – perhaps even seventeenth-century – but agree that it is probably one of the oldest buildings still standing in America. Several other sites have been pointed out as indicating that the Norsemen did explore the new continent further than just its coastline; and these are located in Minnesota, Oklahoma, Ohio, North Dakota, Wisconsin and by the Great Lakes.

The best known artifact in this context is the Kensington Stone, a $2\frac{1}{2}$-foot-high square-shaped block of greywacke stone, with a runic inscription chiselled on two of its sides. It was found on a farm in Kensington in Douglas, County Minnesota, in 1898, and the runic characters allegedly spell out the troubles which beset a party of thirty Norwegians travelling westwards from Vinland on a 'journey of discovery'. It professes to have been written in 1362 as a last desperate message and a memorial to ten of the expedition members who met with violent deaths. Although condemned by many experts as a nineteenth-century fake, the stone has its champions who believe it to be a vital piece of evidence about the Norse journeys in America.

Without doubt the strangest American Viking tale concerns the alleged discovery of a skeleton in a suit of armour early in the last century. This 'find' was immortalized in the poem by Henry Wadsworth Longfellow, *The Skeleton in Armour*. Longfellow wrote his poem after the reported discovery of the skeleton 'clad in broken and corroded armor' at Fall River, near Newport. A somewhat similar discovery was later made in 1828 in the valley of the Black River near the town of Coventry in Vermont. In this case the skeleton wore just a shirt of mail; but again, like its predecessor, it was said to show every sign of being Viking in origin.

The fiercely debated Vinland Map which was acquired by Yale University in 1965 is the other major topic where the Vikings are concerned. This is an ancient world map said to have been drawn by a Swiss monk in 1440 – over fifty years before Columbus sailed to America – and clearly depicting the location of Vinland as North America. Although the map has been rigorously tested and carbon-dated by experts on both sides of the Atlantic – who believe that it is genuine – only recently a group of American ink analysts announced that after studying particles of the map they were convinced it was the work of a twentieth-century forger. This has not shaken the faith of the scholars, however, and Yale experts believe that any modern forger would have to have 'an inconceivable knowledge of medieval maps':[25] so for the moment the positive faction seems to outweigh the negative.

Suggestions that perhaps men from Britain – or at the very least of Celtic origin – reached the continent shortly after the Vikings have been under discussion among American archaeologists following discoveries at a site known appropriately as Mystery Hill near North Salem, New Hampshire.

The sinister altar stone at Mystery Hill near North Salem in New Hampshire, U.S.A.

Here are situated a cluster of twenty-two small dry-walled structures, some with roofs formed by large boulders, others with corbelled vaults. The site has been constantly excavated for many years, and several thousand artifacts dating from many periods and several different cultures have been unearthed. Among these have been a number of stones with inscriptions chiselled on them which, it is being proposed, are in an ancient language called Ogam, used long ago by the Celtic people, whose territories extended from the Scottish Highlands in the north to as far south as Spain. The main supporter of this theory is Dr Barry Fell of Harvard, who has been studying the carvings for some years and says they can be tentatively dated from about 800 BC to the third century AD. He has discovered that traces of these early Celtic settlers fade out at this date, and although it is difficult to discern what their fate might have been, it is possible that they integrated by marriage with the native Red Indians and thereby ceased to exist as an ethnic group.

In a fascinating article published recently, the science fiction writer André Norton raises the idea that this site may have even earlier origins than Celtic – perhaps having first been a Phoenician-Carthaginian settlement. 'In 335 BC,' she writes, 'Aristotle in his list of one hundred and seventy-eight marvels, names as item eighty-four, a mysterious overseas land which the Phoenicians kept a strict secret because of trade. His description as cited might well be that of Mystery Hill. Though, unfortunately, it has been "mined" constantly for the stones which must have made it a most impressive sight a couple of hundred years ago, the remains are unique enough to continue to draw speculation.' Miss Norton confirms the Celtic connection with a further piece of fascinating information: 'It has many features of the well-known Megalithic stonework of Europe and the British Isles – including a sinister altar in proper proportions for human sacrifice, with a speaking tube arrangement through which voices may be eerily projected.'[26]

On the other hand, several archaeologists who have worked at Mystery Hill are opposed to all such ideas, and believe that the site is nothing more than the handiwork of seventeenth- and eighteenth-century colonial farmers; though they admit to being puzzled as to why such undeniably busy men should have bothered to construct edifices of this kind and go to the lengths of inscribing them with obscure symbols.

That redoubtable Scottish seaman Prince Henry Sinclair of the Orkneys, is also associated with the discovery of America – a stone known as the Sinclair Rock at Westford in Massachusetts being claimed to mark one of his landing points on the continent. Prince Henry had long been fired with the idea of finding a great land to the west of his island kingdom, and in 1395 finally launched a small party with himself as leader. According to the records of the voyage kept by a young Italian, Antonio Zeno, the party made several landfalls, but after the loss of a ship Prince Henry sent half his company back to the Orkneys. He apparently stayed on in this unidentified country for a few months before sailing home quite safely. Prince Henry died in 1404 without ever having made clear where his discovery lay. It was not until some years afterwards that the stone at Westford was reported, and at first the markings on it were thought to be Indian. But cleaning and closer inspection revealed the outline of a sword – and the heraldic markings of the Sinclair family. Whether the stone is meant to be a record of the Scottish landing or the burial place of one of the more important members of the party is still open to conjecture.

Perhaps the most intriguing story of Britons landing in America concerns a group of Welsh explorers who allegedly landed in Mobile Bay, Alabama in 1170. They, like the men who were at Mystery Hill, are believed eventually to have ceased to exist as an ethnic group through intermarriage with the Indians. The party, led by the great Prince Madog (or Madoc) ab Owain Gwynedd, had left from North Wales with a fleet of ships and a large contingent of men – accounts of the numbers differed, varying from ten to fifty sailing vessels and between fifty and three hundred crew members. They sailed across the Atlantic, were caught by the North Equatorial current and passed clear through the narrow gap separating Florida from the island of Cuba before making a landfall in what is now Mobile Bay. The mariners settled here, intermarrying with the native Indians and teaching them their own language, until one group was inseparable from the other.

Later, students of anthropology found striking evidence to substantiate this story, both in the numbers of Indians with grey and blue eyes, and the similarity between many local Indian words and those in Welsh. The tribe known as the Mandans who lived on the Missouri were a particular example of this, responding instantly to the Welsh language, using coracles for fishing of a type only found elsewhere in Wales, and becoming white-haired in old

Above left: The earliest
known map with the name
America on it, drawn by
Leonardo da Vinci,
c. 1514 and (*left*) the
famous Zeno map, dated
c. 1400

Above right: An illustration
from Edmond Neukomm's
The Rulers of the Sea
showing Prince Henry
Sinclair with Red Indians

Right: A drawing by
George Catlin of a
Mandan Indian girl

age, a trait no other Indian has shown. Archaeologists researching the same theory were able to locate forts in Tennessee which they said bore strong similarities to those found in Wales. One eighteenth-century French traveller in the area even went as far as to describe the Mandan Indians as 'white men with forts and permanent villages laid out in streets'.[27]

Unfortunately the Mandans were wiped out by a smallpox epidemic in the middle of the nineteenth century, and with them went the living proof of the Welsh landing. But belief in it is strong, as a plaque put up in Mobile Bay in 1953 by the Daughters of the American Revolution graphically states: 'In memory of Prince Madoc, a Welsh explorer who landed on the shores of Mobile Bay in 1170 and left behind, with the Indians, the Welsh language'.

After the exploits of Madoc and those like him, the Middle Ages proved a

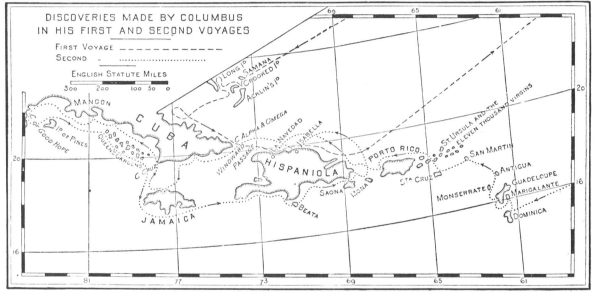

Above: This plan of Columbus's routes appeared in *The Discovery of America* by John Fiske, published in New York in 1892

Right: A rare sketch of Columbus from the Academia real de la Historia de Madrid

54

barren time for exploration; indeed for human endeavour as a whole. It was not, in fact, until the time of Columbus that sea exploration was once more taken up in earnest. That the man from Genoa's voyage should have been crowned with such spectacular success after all those years of indifference is perhaps all the more remarkable.

In conclusion, the only incontrovertible fact that seems to emerge from all this enquiry and speculation is that it could have been just about anyone who reached America first – and the answer will probably never be satisfactorily resolved. Thor Heyerdahl with his incredible trans-Pacific navigation in the balsa craft *Kon Tiki* has proved beyond any reasonable doubt that long voyages in even the most primitive craft are possible and that there may well have been contact between the advanced civilizations in the very earliest times.

A ship of the kind in which Columbus sailed to America, taken from *The Discovery of America by Northmen* by N. Beamish (New York 1841). No engraving of Columbus's actual vessel, the *Hispaniola*, is known to exist

As he has written in *The Quest for America* (1971):

> The speculations as to contacts between the Old World and the New before the voyages of Columbus have never ended. In scientific terms, they have gradually hardened into two opposed schools of thought: Isolationism and Diffusion. The Isolationists believe that the two main oceans surrounding the Americas completely isolated the New World from Old World contact until AD 1492; this school of thought allows only for primitive food gatherers to have passed from the Asiatic tundra to Alaska in the Arctic north. The Diffusionists, in contrast, believe in a single common cradle of all civilisations; they postulate various hypothetical voyages to aboriginal America from Asia, Europe, or Africa in pre-Columbian times.

But none of the argument as to whether Columbus was first to America or not destroys one fundamental truth, adds Thor Heyerdahl. Writing in *Viking America* (1972) he says, 'Did Columbus discover the New World as the textbooks say? He certainly did if we are willing to admit that there were also people ashore on the other side who discovered Columbus when he landed. The meeting of two great worlds was indeed the achievement of Columbus, and Columbus alone. He changed history, both in the Old World, and the New, and history is forever there to prove it.'

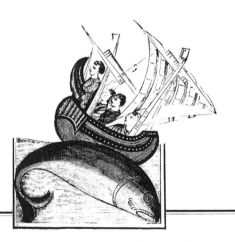

This illustration is taken from N. Beamish's The Discovery of America by Northmen

St Brendan's Voyage to the Americas
An extract from a translation of the sixth-century Latin manuscript, *Navigatio Sancti Brendani,* believed to have been written by St Brendan, in which he describes how his voyage to America began, and also a landfall in the Caribbean where the party took on grapefruit

ST. BRENDAN, having selected fourteen brothers from his own congregation, shut himself up in an oratory with them and spoke to them saying, "My loving fellow warriors I wait advice and help from you because my heart and all my thoughts are united in one desire. Only if it is the will of God, in my heart I propose to search for the Land of the Saints' Promise about which Father

Barinthus spoke. How does it seem to you, or what advice do you wish to give me?"

And they, after learning the desire of the Holy Father, all said as if with one mouth: "Father, your will is our will. Did we not leave our parents, did we not despise our inheritance and did we not surrender our bodies into your hands? And so we are ready to go with you either to death or to life. Let us seek only the will of God."

Therefore, St. Brendan and those who were with him finished Lent, through three days of prayers, and afterwards set out.

After Lent passed and greeted by his brethren and having recommended a Prior of his monastery who was afterward his successor in the same place, he set out toward the western region with fourteen brothers, to the island of a certain Holy Father called Enda. There he tarried for three days and three nights.

After this, having received the blessing of the Holy Father and of all the monks who were with him, he set out into the farthest part of his own region, where his parents resided.

Nevertheless he did not wish to see them, but on the summit of a certain mountain which extended itself far out into the ocean in a place which he called the abode of Brendan's, he set up a tent where there was an inlet for one ship.

St. Brendan and those who were with him after taking iron implements constructed a very lightweight, small vessel, ribbed and columned from the wood which is the custom in those regions, and they covered it with cow hides after they had been tanned.

On the outside they oiled all the junctures of the hides with grease and they emplaced two other boats to be prepared from other hides within the ship.

And with them they took forty days provisions and grease to prepare the hides for the covering of the boat and other utensils which pertain to the use of human life. Also they placed a mast fastened in the centre of the boat and a sail and other things which pertain to the steering of a ship.

Then St. Brendan ordered his brethren in the name of the Father and of the Son and of the Holy Spirit to enter the ship. And St. Brendan himself boarded the boat and after extending the sails began to sail toward the summer sunset. . .

. . . On a certain day they saw an island at a distance from them.

They approached the shore until the ship was beached on the shore. That island was of such a flat surface that it seemed to them that it was level with the sea. It had no trees or anything else which could be moved by the wind. It was very spacious and covered with white and purple scalta.

After the Mass, two of the young men carried a basket full of the fruit and went into the boat saying, "Take of the fruit of the island of strong men."

St. Brendan began to sail with his comrades. When it was time he ordered his brethren to refresh their bodies with the fruit, and he took one of the fruits. As soon as he saw its size and how full of juice it was, he wondered and said, "Never have I seen or read of a fruit of such size." For they were of equal size in the manner of a large pile.

Then St. Brendan ordered a water vessel be brought to him and he opened one of the fruits and brought forth one pound of the juice which he divided into twelve measures and gave to each brother a single measure.

So for twelve days, the brothers were refreshed from each fruit, always retaining in their mouths the taste of honey.

IV
THE STONE COMPUTERS

Sunset at the mysterious Legananny Dolmen at
Dromara in Northern Ireland

SCATTERED across the British Isles are more than 900 groups of standing stones, many in circles and all dating from prehistoric times. These megaliths are mostly placed in isolated and dramatic locations, a fact which has helped to stimulate centuries of debate as to their meaning and purpose. Opinions have varied, some regarding them as having religious significance as sacrificial places; the most recent and exciting theory is that many of them were Stone Age computers.

The raising of huge stones of this kind is by no means restricted to the British Isles – similar examples are to be found in France, Egypt, South America and even Japan – and all appear to have been part of a cultural development that took place at certain periods all over the world. For most people the simple explanation as to their use seems to have been that they were the work of priestly orders; in Britain the Druids have for a long time been popularly associated with the megaliths and their use.

What is beyond dispute is the skill that went into the erection and siting of the stones and circles, and it was this which became the basis of the revolutionary theory that they had been exactly laid out with a standard measuring instrument and were to perform, in effect, the complex role of being astronomical observatories for the sun and moon. At a stroke, the theorists, led by Professor Alexander Thom, claimed that men of the early Bronze Age were highly skilled surveyors, builders and astronomers – capable of constructing right-angled triangles, circles, flattened circles, egg-shapes and even ellipses. Long before Pythagoras, they knew the basic principles of geometry. As the renowned archaeologist Dr Euan MacKie has written, 'It looks as if our early Bronze Age society included an intellectual class with undreamed of capabilities in practical surveying, geometry and astronomy, and with the power and prestige to command large labour forces to erect thousands of heavy stones in the situations and formations they wanted, all over the British Isles.'[28]

The stone constructions in the British Isles began to be built from 4000 BC onwards, when the country was being colonized by a race of Neolithic farmers who, unlike the resident population, also possessed the ability to make simple stone tools for agricultural use. Once established, they developed their skill over the years, graduating from simple burial grounds and earthen barrows to the full-blown megaliths and stone circles we can see today.

After over thirty years of research, Professor Thom has come to the conclusion that the idea behind these stone circles and groups was basically a very

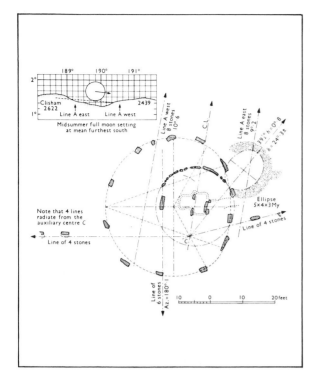

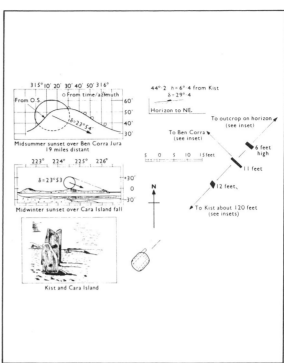

The layout and alignment, relative to the sun and moon, of two important Scottish sites – the Callanish stones (*left*) and Ballochroy – from *Megalithic Sites in Britain* by Professor A. Thom (London 1967)

practical one: man wanted a calendar that he could use for agricultural and domestic purposes. By studying the stones, the Professor has demonstrated that many of them give precise bearings on the sun and major star movements at various times of the year, while others can chart the moon through its various phases.

To support his theory, Professor Thom established that a uniform measurement applied to all the constructions, and he tested this out against 150 stone circles from the south of England to the north of Scotland. This measurement, which he has called a 'Megalithic Yard', was exactly 2·72 feet, and when he applied it to the stones he found such minute differences that he was forced to conclude that impressively sophisticated instruments must have been employed to attain such uniformity.

How the 'Megalithic Yard' was originally arrived at is a subject of some controversy among experts. It has been suggested that the basic measurement of this time may have been related to the average height of megalithic man – 5·44 feet – but the figure which Professor Thom has derived from calculations made against the distances between the standing stones seems the most workable.

Research has also shown that many of these stones are aligned with particular points on the horizon and even in some cases with one another. This has led to the conclusion by investigators like T. C. Lethbridge, who is both an archaeologist and a psychic researcher, that they may all be linked in a system that once transmitted a powerful life force across the countryside for the benefit of the land and the people who lived on it. Mr Lethbridge maintains that this system has long since fallen into disuse, but occasional experiments on such sites have resulted in electric shocks being felt by those involved and photographs produced which show inexplicable light radiations emanating from the stones.

A great many of the megaliths are decorated with carved designs – especially the 'cup-and-rings' variety – and again study has shown that they are set out with mathematical accuracy. They may well have served some practical purpose, but could just as easily have been magical marks of some kind.

The evidence which has been collected on those sites used for ceremonial purposes dates them to the middle and late Neolithic period. Professor MacKie explains this particular aspect of our story:

> The "henge" monuments – whether of wood or stone – were circular enclosures, with either one or two entrances and defined by a ditch with a bank outside it. A fortified site always has an external ditch, but the arrangement in the henge suggests a ritual demarcation of a circular sacred area. In Southern England some henges had, inside the boundary ditches, elaborate circular settings of wooden posts which were very probably roofed buildings. These could easily have been temples. And recent work at Durrington Walls has yielded not only several such circular settings, but also large quantities of domestic refuse, suggesting that the site was not only a ceremonial centre, but also a residential area for priests and novices – wooden British equivalents of the Maya Neolithic stone ceremonial sites of central America. [29]

The most famous of the sites in Britain is unquestionably Stonehenge, which is often erroneously associated with the magical rites of the Druids, who were supposed to have built it. In fact it is older than Druidism, and was probably only commandeered by members of that cult.

This massive, eerie construction rising from Salisbury Plain remains to this day one of the great enigmas of legend, the source of endless folk tales, and the topic of continuing scientific study. A persistent legend says that it is a memorial to a group of British nobles who were treacherously slaughtered by the Saxons and that it was raised on the advice of Merlin with magical stones brought from Ireland. Another story credits the Devil with its construction – as nothing more than a puzzle to humanity!

It was the seventeenth-century antiquarian and gossip writer John Aubrey who first really brought Stonehenge to public notice and suggested the connection with the Druids which has persisted to this day. It was also this association which led to two of the largest fallen stones being named the 'Slaughter Stone' and the 'Altar Stone' in memory of supposed bloody sacrifices. Other 'experts' have named the original builders as being men from Gaul, Phoenicians or the Romans themselves! (This last suggestion was the considered opinion of the man who conducted what can be counted as the first investigation of the stones, the architect Inigo Jones, who was given the task by James I.)

The facts of the matter are that Stonehenge was built in three stages, the

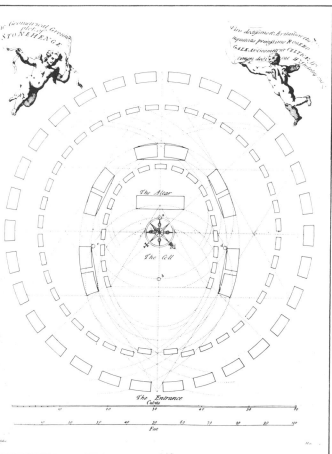

Top: The majesty of Stonehenge

Far left: An engraving of a British Druid and
(*left*) a geometrical plan of Stonehenge, both from
William Stukeley's *Stonehenge: A Temple
Restor'd to the British Druids* (London 1740)

Above: The raising of a stone at Stonehenge during
excavations carried out in 1901, an illustration
from Sir Norman Lockyer's *Stonehenge and Other
British Stone Monuments Astronomically Considered*
(London 1909)

first builders being the Neolithic people who, around 2600 BC, constructed the outer ditch and bank and the circle of fifty-six holes, two to four feet deep, known as the Aubrey Holes after their discoverer. Eight hundred years later the 'Beaker People' – so named because of the pottery they buried with their dead – carried out the massive task of erecting sixty bluestones, each weighing four tons, in a double circle. These stones, research has established, had been brought all the way from the Prescelly Hills in Wales by a feat of engineering that almost defies belief. The Beaker People also raised an avenue of earth banks almost two miles long stretching from Stonehenge to the River Avon. The final stage of development of the circle was undertaken by the Wessex people during the fifteenth century BC, when the older bluestones were uprooted and the sarsen blocks, which are such a familiar feature, put up. These huge stones, up to twenty-one feet in height and weighing fifty tons, had been brought to the site from about twenty miles to the north in Wiltshire. The inner and outer rings of these uprights and lintels probably gave rise to the Saxon name 'hanging stones', from which 'Stonehenge' almost certainly derived. In any event, it remains an undisputed fact that Stonehenge was never quite completed by any of three groups who developed it, and the reason for this must forever remain a mystery.

The awe in which people hold Stonehenge can only be increased by considering the effort that went into its construction. As Kenneth B. Platnick wrote in his *Great Mysteries of History* (1971), 'The project, after all, took half a millennium to bring to completion. It required, according to one recent calculation, no fewer than $1\frac{1}{2}$ million man-days of labour. (That's more than 40 men working around the clock for 100 years.) It required the ingenuity to transport those heavy stones over land and sea for distances of hundreds of miles. It required the expenditure of a large portion of community wealth that might well have been spent otherwise.'

In this context, Professor Gerald S. Hawkins, an American astronomer who has contributed much of the most important evidence that Stonehenge was a prehistoric computer, has written, 'The American Space Programme takes about one per cent of our gross national product; Stonehenge must have taken at least a corresponding amount. Their building effort may have required more of them than our Space Programme does of us; correspondingly, it could have meant much more to them.'[30]

It was in 1961 that Professor Hawkins collected together data on the immense number of alignments that could be found between the courses of the sun and moon and the various stones and arches of Stonehenge, and fed all this information into a computer. This, he hoped, would give a clue to the purpose of the construction. He as much as anyone was amazed when the results clearly indicated that Stonehenge had been built as a huge observatory for following the movements of the two heavenly bodies and capable of making highly intricate astronomical calculations, including predictions of equinoctial sunrises and sunsets, moonrises and moonsets, and even eclipses. Professor Hawkins's report has since been the subject of much discussion,

'A peep into the Sanctum Sanctorum', another superb engraving from Stukeley's *Stonehenge*

but it is now gaining wider acceptance and may well take us closer to solving the enigma of Stonehenge.

After Stonehenge, the huge earthwork and circle of ancient stones that surrounds the village of Avebury, some seventeen miles to the north, is probably the most famous in the British Isles. It is certainly the largest henge monument. There is little point in comparing the two constructions, though John Aubrey, who was also responsible for popularizing Avebury, wrote, 'It does as much exceed in greatness the so renowned Stonehenge as a Cathedral doeth a parish church.' Aubrey described the site quite simply as 'a double circle of stones, four or five foot high, though most of them are now fallen down'.[31]

Another antiquarian, William Stukeley, who published the first detailed studies on both Stonehenge and Avebury in the early eighteenth century, also believed erroneously that Avebury had been built by the Druids, but was the first to realize that the circle was only part of a larger shape like that of a giant serpent. Unfortunately, Stukeley's views that snake worship had gone on here were later derided, but his plans and sketches made while desecration was going on all around have proved of considerable value to experts. Because of opinions like his – and they were far from new – it is perhaps not surprising to learn that the Church had much of the site levelled and the stones over-turned, and it has only been in this century that the construction has been restored to anything like its former glory.

Avebury is undoubtedly older than Stonehenge, and is believed to have been built as a sun temple. With its circle and its two avenues of stones each a mile and a half long the site was far more complex than Stonehenge. Originally there were 100 stones in the main circle but the number is now a mere 27; in the avenue there were 200, but only a fraction remain. The Church was not solely responsible for this; local farmers and the inhabitants of the district also ploughed up the site and removed much of the stonework for building and other purposes. Nonetheless, it has been possible to re-mark the serpent shape Stukeley mapped, which probably symbolized the supreme creative power of the sun matched with the inner wisdom of mankind.

Right: John Aubrey, a sketch in the Ashmolean Museum

Opposite: The layout of Avebury, from William Stukeley's *Abury, A Temple of the British Druids* (London 1743)

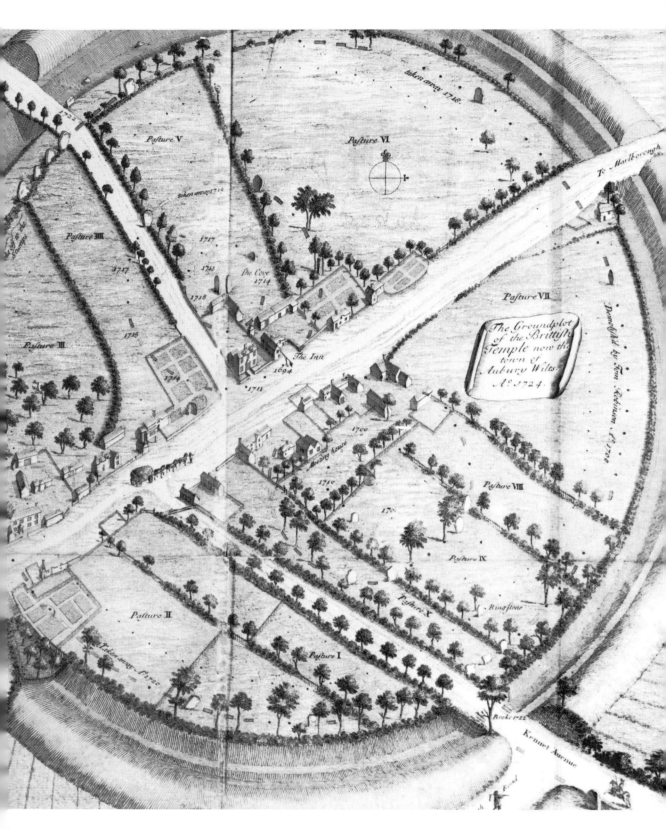

Pasture V

taken away 1718.

Pasture VI

To Marlborough

Pasture III

taken away 1718

1717

1717

1718

1715

1718

The Cove
1714

Pasture III

1714

1711

The Inn

1694

Pasture VII

Pasture VIII

Demolish by Tom Robinson L⁴ 1700

The Groundplot
of the Brittish
Temple now the
town of
Aubury Wilts
A°. 1724.

Berkhouse

1700

1710

Pasture II

176

taken away 1710

Pasture IX

Pasture I

Pasture X

Ringstone

Broken 1722

Kennet Avenue

Right: The Callanish stones in the Outer Hebrides

Opposite: The Ring of Brogar on the Orkney mainland

Below: The stone circle at Avebury

There are numerous other ancient stone circles in the British Isles associated with the 'computer' theory, and I should like to mention one or two of the more important areas here, although the interested reader is directed to the various other more detailed studies, in particular Professor Thom's own seminal works, *Megalithic Sites in Britain* (1967) and *Megalithic Lunar Observatories* (1971).

The most mysterious of all the sites is certainly the group of standing stones at Callanish on the Isle of Lewis in the Outer Hebrides. A more remote and desolate spot would be hard to imagine. The stones are laid in the form of a giant cross; the centrepiece of the design is a circle of thirteen tall pillars, in the middle of which stands a lone pillar, or menhir, nearly sixteen feet tall. From this circle there is an avenue of nineteen double stones to the north, about 270 feet long – seeming to form an approach way – a short row of four stones forming a 'head' to the south, and two 'arms' projecting at right angles. Scattered throughout the vicinity are various megalithic sites, and it was these that the astronomer Boyle T. Somerville linked with Callanish in 1912 to suggest that it had been an astronomical observatory. It was the work of this man and his published findings that were later to inspire Professor Alexander Thom to formulate his more advanced theory of a nationwide complex of stone computers. The completeness of the site at Callanish has also helped both Professor Thom and Gerald S. Hawkins to test many of their sun and moon theories originally arising from their study of Stonehenge.

Another isolated site which Professor Thom found significant was the Ring of Brogar, a megalithic circle not unlike that at Avebury and sited on a strip of land between two lochs at Stennes on the Orkney mainland. The picturesquely sited circle measures 340 feet across and has twenty-seven

standing pillars remaining from an original total of sixty. In the district there are also numerous cairns and tombs which Professor Thom believes were used by the Neolithic builders for their astronomy – though what remains puzzling here, as at Callanish, is why such a deserted spot should have proved so suitable for such a major undertaking. One is tempted to conclude that there was probably some kind of centre of population here all those centuries ago.

The two other Scottish sites which experts believe most convincingly support Professor Thom's theory are at Ballochroy, on the west coast of Kintyre, and Kintraw in Argyll. They are sited close enough together for regular communication, and share the Jura mountains as a common focal point for astronomical observation. As Evan Hadingham has noted in *Circles and Standing Stones* (1975), 'These two sites could well represent the means by which a precise calendar system, probably used in other parts of early Britain, was established and kept in phase with the sun's movements.'

At Ballochroy there is a large megalithic cist which may well have covered a communal burial ground, and aligned with it about one hundred feet away are three large, flat-faced stones. Even the most cursory glance shows how the whole arrangement can be aligned, on the one hand with the outline of Cara Island, where the winter sun sets, and on the other with the more distant rounded peaks of the Juras, where the midsummer sun passes. With its provisions for charting these two key points of the solar calendar, and by inference those in between, the Ballochroy site is of paramount importance in Professor Thom's theory.

The Kintraw site is about 35 miles north of Ballochroy and consists of a twelve-foot-high standing stone and the remains of a cairn. There were probably other constructions, too, but even the existing remains were enough to show Professor Thom how crucial sun changes could be correlated with significant changes in the shapes of the Jura mountains. Important work on this site has been carried out recently by Dr Euan MacKie, who has established that there was originally a kind of observation 'terrace' and also another large stone forming, with the existing menhir, a 'wedge shape' through which the winter solstice could have been accurately observed.

Some mention should also be made of the Irish stone circles, of which there is an important concentration around Lough Gur in County Limerick. The main circle consists of a ring of stones, in the middle of which stands a massive fourteen-foot-high rectangular stone, some four feet thick by seven feet wide. This site, like several of the others, has definitely been attributed to the workmanship of the Beaker People because of the pottery remnants unearthed there. It has been claimed that Lough Gur is as important a construction as Avebury in England, although some experts think the most significant of all Irish sites was at Roscrea in County Tipperary, where about three hundred upright stones once stood in a dazzling configuration – until the area was plundered in the 1930s for road-making materials!

Perhaps, finally, the most intriguing of all the stone circles is the one to be found at Arbor Low in Derbyshire. I say intriguing because this site, about five miles from the town of Bakewell and almost a thousand feet up on the Derbyshire moors, bears an almost uncanny resemblance to a clock face when viewed from above. With only one exception, all the large stones in the circle are lying flat, and it is debatable whether they ever did stand upright. Astronomers, archaeologists and students of mysterious phenomena are much puzzled by this construction – the last-named group conjecturing that the site may once have been a centre of natural energy, as some fifty 'ley' lines are said to link with it. Whatever the truth, its importance in the general thesis about astronomical measurement in the British Isles would seem likely to be a major one.

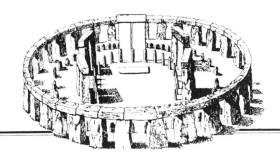

Stonehenge 'restored', a drawing by Sir Thomas Browne from *The Druids* by T. D. Kendrick (London 1927)

Stonehenge – An Astronomical Observatory
An extract from *Beyond Stonehenge* by Gerald S. Hawkins, London 1973

IN RECENT years the archaeological knowledge concerning Stonehenge in Wiltshire, England, had reached a level of detail sufficient to encourage other disciplines to attempt to investigate the purpose of the structure. Radiocarbon dating and other archaeological evidence indicate that the work at Stonehenge began around 2000 BC with the digging of a ditch and holes. This date is uncertain by a century or so, and is based on the radiocarbon dating of a charcoal fragment using the revised half-life for C_{14}. The erection of the stone parts of Stonehenge, the trilithon archways, sarsen circle, etc., commenced about 1700 BC. It was possible to show that even though building and rebuilding lasted at the site for several centuries, the post holes, stones, and archways continued to align with the rising and setting of the extreme positions of the sun and moon on the horizon. The sun, of course, would touch these extreme positions during one tropical year, but the moon would require 18.6 years to complete a cycle. Thus it seemed evident that Stonehenge, built and rebuilt by different cultural groups, had a consistent astronomical building plan throughout the period.

Archaeological excavations established the number of holes in the various circles that had been dug and subsequently refilled, either by natural causes or by man. The numbers in the circles were very significant from the astronomical point of view. A circle of 29 holes and a circle of 30 holes seemed to represent the long and short synodic months of ancient calendars. The 56 Aubrey holes could well represent a seasonal eclipse cycle. It was therefore suggested that the circles at Stonehenge were used for computing the phases of the moon and also for predicting the month of the year in which eclipses would take place.

The determination that Stonehenge was an elaborate astronomical observatory and the suggestion that it was also a computer resulted from a direct interaction of the two disciplines of astronomy and archaeology, and the resultant merging was called "astro-archaeology." The field of research fits well within the topic of the history of science in general, or the history of astronomy in particular – that is, if one is willing to overlook the rigorous definition of history as resulting from the written word. Stonehenge is wordless and correctly belongs to prehistoric times, but perhaps the reading of information from alignments of stones and the number of holes in various circles can be regarded as information retrieval analogous to reading. It is the unwritten evidence, the prehistory of science.

The notion that early man made astronomical observations was quite prevalent in early folklore, though unproved. Stukeley (1740) remarks on the fact that the principal line of the whole Stonehenge work points to the northeast, "whereabouts the Sun rises, when the days are longest." From the context of this sentence it appears that Stukeley, even in 1740, was claiming no originality for this suggestion. The Gaelic people of Scotland seem always to have referred to the fact that the many stone circles in that part of the world pointed in some way to the sun. In 1893 Magnus Spence suggested sun and moon alignments for the stones and burial chambers near Maeshowe in the Orkneys, and detailed calculations have later shown that some of his suggestions were correct. Sir Norman Lockyer demonstrated that the axis of Stonehenge points to the mid-summer sunrise and used this fact to establish an archaeological date (Lockyer and Penrose, 1901). Lockyer suggested several alignments for other megalithic structures in the British Isles, and also alignments with certain stars. According to him, most of the temples in Egypt and Greece were aligned to point to the rising or setting of certain stars. Recently Thom (1965) has discussed the intricate geometrical basis for megalithic structures in the British Isles and suggested solar, lunar, and stellar alignments among the stones and stone circles.

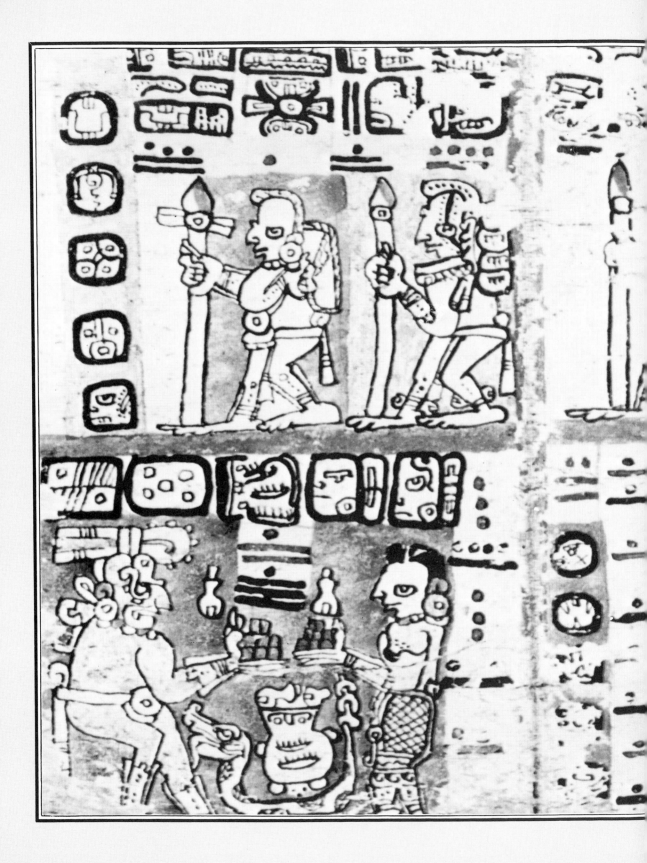

V

SUBMERGED
CONTINENTS

The Troana Codex, an ancient Mayan manuscript
said to record the destruction of the continent of
Mu

LEGENDS of sunken worlds – lands and even whole continents deluged by flood or catastrophe – feature strongly in the traditions of several nations, some based on fact, others on old tales of fantasy and imagination. While modern science is unable to support the idea of a universal deluge, investigators agree that even stories like the Great Flood in the Bible probably have some basis in actual occurrence. They cite instances like the terrible devastation of Lisbon in 1775 when, in under six minutes, half the city slid into the Atlantic and 60,000 lives were lost; or the volcanic explosion of Krakatoa in 1883 when tidal waves crossed the entire Pacific, destroyed 295 towns and killled 36,000 people. Such occurrences are by no means uncommon in history, and for an earlier and more susceptible people might well with the passing of years have taken on the aura of legendary or religious significance.

It is interesting to note, as Sir James Frazer pointed out in his *Folklore in the Old Testament* (1918), that while flood legends are numerous and clearly recorded among the races of the Mediterranean basin, they are vague further north or south and practically nonexistent in China and Australia. This would indicate their focal point to have been the mid-Atlantic, and suggests a genuine historical origin for the legendary submergence of several nations, including the most famous of all, the fabled Atlantis.

The legend of Atlantis has for centuries been a source of endless fascination for scientists and layman alike: indeed, according to a recent estimation by Colonel A. Braghine in his book *The Shadow of Atlantis* (1968), there are over 25,000 volumes dedicated to Atlantology in various languages! The very word Atlantis evokes for everyone the idea of an advanced civilization, existing in utopian conditions, finally overwhelmed in the year 9600 BC by a combination of increasing decadence and fantastic cataclysm. The background to the story, as the passage of time has shown, lies partly in fact and partly in fiction, and such is the popular desire to solve the mystery that recently a group of English newspapermen voted the re-emergence of Atlantis as the fourth most important news story they could imagine – five places ahead of the Second Coming of Christ!

The first existing account of Atlantis is to be found in the writings of the Greek philosopher Plato, in the fourth century BC. It has, however, been suggested that if the great library at Alexandria, which contained millions of irreplaceable papyri providing a coverage of all ancient knowledge, had not

Above: Atlantis as seen by the seventeenth-century scholar Athanasius Kircher

Right: A recent drawing of the city of Atlantis as it is described in Plato's *Critias*

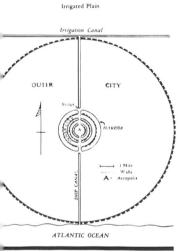

Irrigated Plain

been burned to the ground there would have been numerous other even earlier accounts of the lost continent available to us.

Plato sets forward the basic story of Atlantis in two dialogues, *Timaeus* and *Critias*, basing his account on the reports brought from Egypt by the once exiled Athenian lawmaker Solon, considered one of the wisest men of antiquity. Solon had heard the story from a group of Egyptian priests who said that the empire of Atlantis had been centred on an island west of the Pillars of Herakles (now the Straits of Gibraltar), and was larger than North Africa and Asia Minor combined. The Atlanteans had apparently become greedy to extend their empire and had carried their conquest as far as Egypt and Tuscany before they were defeated by the resolute Athenians. Then followed the great earthquake and flood which annihilated the Athenian army but also plunged Atlantis below the waves. Solon, so it is said, had intended to write a long narrative poem based on the story, but the pressure of politics prevented this: the tale was then handed down through his family until Plato committed it to paper, no doubt embellishing it somewhat in the process.

According to Plato, Atlantis was rich in vegetation and minerals, a land intensively cultivated, technologically advanced and ruled by a federation of ten kings. At the heart of the empire was the city of Atlantis, set on the south coast of the continent, and consisting of a circular metropolis about fifteen miles in diameter. In the centre was a hill on which stood the lavish royal palace and a temple, and around this hill rings of land and water all connected by a system of tunnels and bridges. On the outer ring were enormous docks, and beyond the city a huge plain, served by hot and cold water springs, which was divided up into farming lots. Although Plato gives further details of the style of Atlantean civilization and its achievements, he makes no mention of the explosives, searchlights and even aircraft which have been credited to these people by some enthusiastic modern students of the legend!

In examining Plato's story there are several immediate discrepancies which do undermine its credibility, such as the battles between the Atlanteans and the Athenians in 9600 BC, which would have taken place before there were any Athenians; the existence of farming at a time at least 2,500 years before the earliest farming communities; and the construction of monumental architecture of a kind not recorded anywhere before 4000 BC. Nevertheless if one allows for exaggeration and error, there is much, historians agree, that seems to be historical fact.

Support is also given to Plato's story by the striking similarities between the religions, social customs and architectures of the peoples living on opposite sides of the Atlantic. Several authorities have pointed out that although Central America and the Mediterranean basin are separated by 3,500 miles of ocean, yet the cultures of Egypt and Peru, Phoenicia and Mexico are similar to a degree that makes it seem that they had a common origin. Yet all traces of the great people from whom they might have derived their civilization have vanished from the earth.

For a time after Plato's death there was much speculation among his pupils and then later philosophers about the story of Atlantis; the consensus of opinion was summed up by Aristotle, who said that 'he who invented it also destroyed it'.[32] This attitude was not shared by everyone, and indeed the legend took on the aura of fact in the later Roman Empire, but such scepticism may well account for the lack of any substantial mention of the lost continent during the following three centuries.

The story was not revived until the Middle Ages, when European man began speculating on the possibility of lands beyond the known oceans. There was much that was ridiculous about this speculation – like the stories of the island of the Anthropophagi, 'the men whose heads do grow beneath their shoulders'[33] – but serious exploration did also take place, culminating in the great voyage of Christopher Columbus. Following his triumph, rumours of lost continents throughout the Atlantic began to proliferate, and maps of the time – such as Ortelius's grand 'World Map' of 1570 – showed imaginary lands in a host of unlikely locations.

The man mainly responsible for reviving the Atlantis story was the Spanish historian Francesco López de Gomara, who suggested in his *General History of the Indies* (1533) that the America found by Columbus was the same continent as Plato's. The Greek philosopher, he said, might somehow have heard tales of an Atlantic continent and based his story upon them. This was the spark needed to make the legend flare into life again, and soon both geographers and historians were busy trying to demonstrate that Atlantis and America were indeed one and the same. The French cartographer Sanson, for instance, published a map in 1689 showing how America/Atlantis had been divided up by the federation of ten kings, and the English philosopher Sir Francis Bacon began expounding the idea in his unfinished romance *The New Atlantis*. The

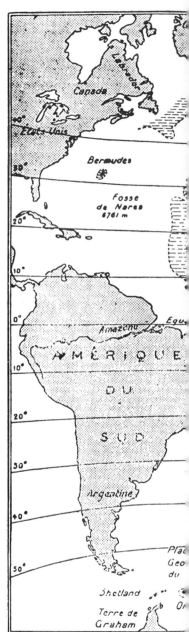

Left: The 'Atlantis in America' theory was partly based on burial mounds such as this one in Caldwell County, North Carolina – an illustration from *Mound Explorations* by C. Thomas, published in America in 1897

Above: A nineteenth-century French concept of the extent of Atlantis which appeared in the magazine *Atlantide* in 1869

strongest advocate was perhaps the historian John Swain, who wrote in his *Speculum Mundi* (1644) that, 'I think [it] may be supposed that America was sometime part of that great land which Plato calleth the Atlantick island, and that the Kings of that island had some intercourse between the people of Europe and Africa.' Swain believed that when the island sank it first became a sea of mud, and as such unnavigable; it was therefore avoided and gradually faded from memory. Nevertheless, he added, 'Yet that such an island was, and swallowed by an earthquake, I am verily perswaded: and if America joyned not to the West part of it, yet surely it could not be farre distant, because Plato describes it as a great island.'

This theory seems to have held ground for another two hundred years, the last important speculator being the German poet Robert Prutz, who in 1855 not only located Atlantis in America but offered an extensive thesis proving that the Phoenicians had actually been the first to find the continent.

It was perhaps only appropriate that the man who a few years later first brought scientific fact and well-argued theory to bear on the Atlantis theory should have been an American, and that he should have disposed of the idea that his homeland had been the original Atlantis with well-marshalled data and the damning indictment that American civilization had barely advanced beyond barbarism in Plato's time and could certainly never have carried out military campaigns across the ocean. This remarkable man was Ignatius Donnelly (1831–1901), a former lawyer, journalist and Congressman (he also twice ran for Vice-President) whose study of ancient documents was to earn him the epithet 'perhaps the most erudite man ever to sit in the House of Representatives'.[34] From this study came *Atlantis: The Antediluvian World*, first published in 1882 and subsequently running to close on a hundred printings. As this whole work, and much of the cult of Atlantism which has followed, was based on thirteen theses proposed by Donnelly, they are worth repeating in full:

1. That there once existed in the Atlantic Ocean, opposite the mouth of the Mediterranean Sea, a large island, which was the remnant of an Atlantic continent, and known to the ancient world as Atlantis.

2. That the description of this island given by Plato is not, as has long been supposed, fable, but veritable history.

3. That Atlantis was the region where man first rose from a state of barbarism to civilization.

4. That it became, in the course of ages, a populous and mighty nation, from whose overflowings the shores of the Gulf of Mexico, the Mississippi River, the Amazon, the Pacific coast of South America, the Mediterranean, the west coast of Europe and Africa, the Baltic, the Black Sea, and the Caspian were populated by civilized nations.

5. That it was the true Antediluvian World; the Garden of Eden; the Garden of the Hesperides; the Elysian Fields; the Garden of Alcinous; the Mesomphalos; the Olympos; the Asgard of the traditions of the ancient nations; representing a universal memory of a great land, where early

77

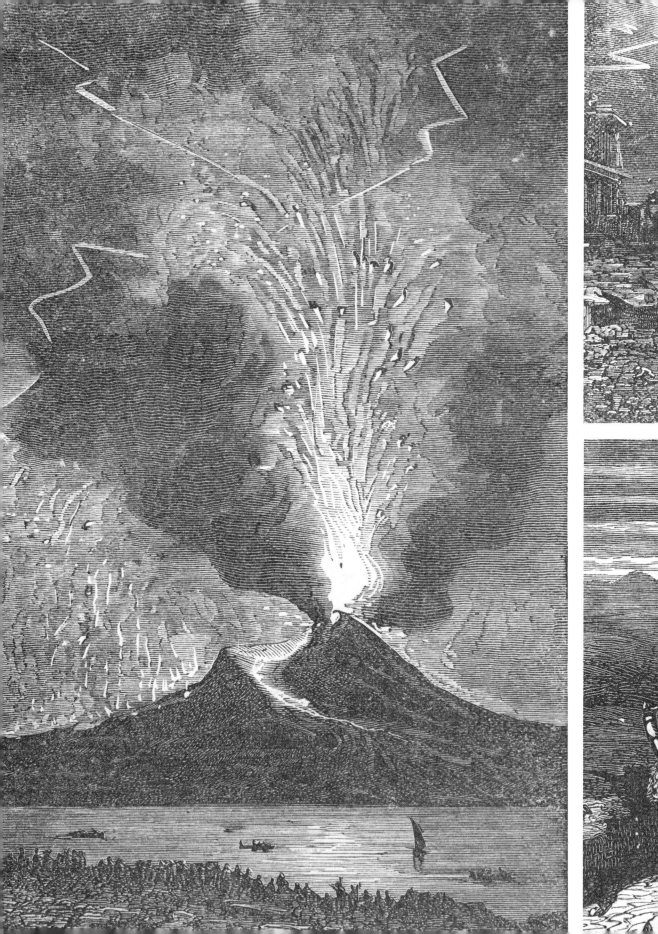

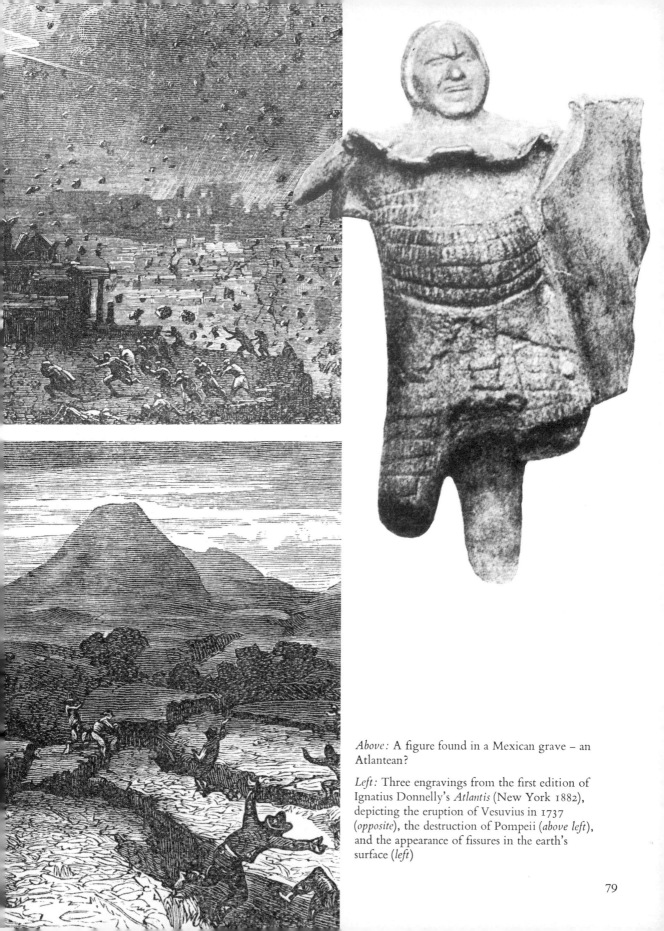

Above: A figure found in a Mexican grave – an Atlantean?

Left: Three engravings from the first edition of Ignatius Donnelly's *Atlantis* (New York 1882), depicting the eruption of Vesuvius in 1737 (*opposite*), the destruction of Pompeii (*above left*), and the appearance of fissures in the earth's surface (*left*)

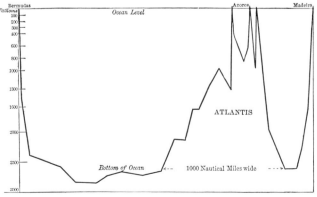

mankind dwelt for ages in peace and happiness.

6. That the gods and goddesses of the ancient Greeks, the Phoenicians, the Hindus and the Scandinavians were simply the kings, queens, and heroes of Atlantis; and the acts attributed to them in mythology are a confused recollection of real historical events.

7. That the mythology of Egypt and Peru represented the original religion of Atlantis, which was sun worship.

8. That the oldest colony formed by the Atlanteans was probably in Egypt, whose civilization was a reproduction of that of the Atlantic island.

9. That the implements of the Bronze Age of Europe were derived from Atlantis. The Atlanteans were also the first manufacturers of iron.

10. That the Phoenician alphabet, parent of all the European alphabets, was derived from an Atlantean alphabet, which was also conveyed from Atlantis to the Mayas of Central America.

11. That Atlantis was the original seat of the Aryan or Indo-European family of nations, as well as the Semitic peoples, and possibly also of the Turanian races.

12. That Atlantis perished in a terrible convulsion of nature, in which the whole island sank into the ocean with nearly all its inhabitants.

13. That a few persons escaped in ships and on rafts, and carried to the nations east and west tidings of the appalling catastrophe, which has survived to our own time in the Flood and Deluge legends of the different nations of the old and new worlds.

On these planks was Donnelly's book built and he argued each point with conviction and an erudite use of widely differing source material. All Atlantis books since, whatever their viewpoint, draw heavily on his lead, and any study of the legend confers on his work an importance comparable with that of Plato's dialogues. (It is interesting to note that no less a person than the British prime minister Gladstone was persuaded by Donnelly's argument and tried unsuccessfully to raise the money for a British expedition to find Atlantis!)

While, on the one hand, still more extraordinary theories have continued to be advanced by groups of Atlantean enthusiasts (some of an occult leaning claim to be in touch with the souls of dead Atlanteans), the development of sophisticated geological dating techniques plus advances in underwater exploration have enabled scientific work to be carried out on locations suggested as being those where Atlantis might have stood. The traditional idea that the lost continent was in the middle of the Atlantic has now made way for other proposals which place it variously in the region of Heligoland, Tunisia, south-western Spain, north-western France and in the area now covered by the Caspian Sea. This last idea, proposed by a group of Russian scientists, is based on the flimsy argument that primitive man was rarely able to accurately locate anything at sea, and quite simply put Atlantis in the wrong place! (A strong case has also been advanced that the site was in the vicinity of Bimini in the Bahamas following the underwater discovery in February 1969 by two

Atlantean architecture on both sides of the Atlantic? *Opposite above:* Treasure house at Mycenae, Greece and (*above*) the arch of Las Monjas at Palenque in Central America

Opposite below: The profile and the extent of the empire of Atlantis according to Ignatius Donnelly

young American writers, Michael Grumley and Robert Ferro, of a 700-yard section of what was believed to be a 31-mile series of massive sea walls stretching around the island. Later expeditions during that year located a series of broken sections of forty-four pillars, hand carved from stone indigenous to the Andes. Preliminary tests suggest that the date of the massive sea-wall stones, some of which are twenty feet across, is 9500 BC – the date given by Plato for the destruction of Atlantis.)

The end-product of all this work is a theoretical site for Atlantis which both stands up to stringent scientific examination and almost literally vindicates Plato's age-old story. The location is based upon the small, crescent-shaped island of Thira (sometimes referred to by its Italian name of Santorini) seventy miles north of Crete. It has now been established that Thira is in fact the ruin of a major volcano and that this once blew up in a cataclysmic eruption which caused the downfall of Minoan Crete and affected most of the Aegean Sea.

In the 1960s a Greek seismologist, Angelous Galanopoulos, connected the eruption of Thira with Plato's Atlantis, and in a book written with Edward Bacon, *Atlantis* (1969), explained his theory:

> For some years now it has been apparent to scholars that the Atlantis described by Plato was very like what archaeology has uncovered of the High Bronze Age civilisations of the Aegean and the Near East – such as the Minoans, the Mycenaeans, the Hittites, the Egyptians and the Babylonians – between about 2500 and 1200 BC. Was there, then, something wrong with Plato's date? Had the Egyptian priests or Solon confused 900 with 9000 years? If so, the date of the disaster would be 1500 BC instead of 9600 BC.
>
> This hypothesis immediately makes the Atlantean civilisation credible. Again, if there is a mistake with the power of ten here, it could apply equally to the large dimensions given for the empire of Atlantis. If so, the dimensions for the Royal City of Atlantis shrink to something very closely approximating to the central plain of Crete (the heartland of the Minoan civilisation) and the date of the disaster to around 1500 BC, the time, nearly enough, that the Minoan empire collapsed in a series of disasters which led to the Mycenaean take-over. Furthermore, Minoan Crete was a prosperous power in close contact with both Athens and Egypt, both of which were then in existence.
>
> Was there a natural cataclysm which took place in the Aegean around this date? There was indeed: the world's greatest known volcanic explosion, that of the island volcano of Santorin, some 70 miles north of Crete. . . .

In 1967 Galanopoulos's theory received valuable support as a result of excavations carried out on Thira by a Professor Marinatos of Athens who located actual Minoan remains beneath pumice deposits. Two years later the leading Atlantologist J. V. Luce published his book *The End of Atlantis*, in which he studied in detail the similarities between the demise of Thera and the fall of Atlantis and added his considerable weight to the proposal that the fabled Atlantis had at last been found. But whether science will ever completely transform the magic of Atlantis into accepted fact perhaps only time will tell.

Atlantis is not, of course, the only sunken land of tradition; there are

The Greek island of Thira is now being proposed as the origin of the Atlantis legend. *Above:* One of the actively volcanic 'Burnt Islands' situated off Thira and (*opposite above*) the lava- and pumice-covered cliffs of Thira

Right: Pots found during excavations at Akrotiri on the Greek island of Samothraki

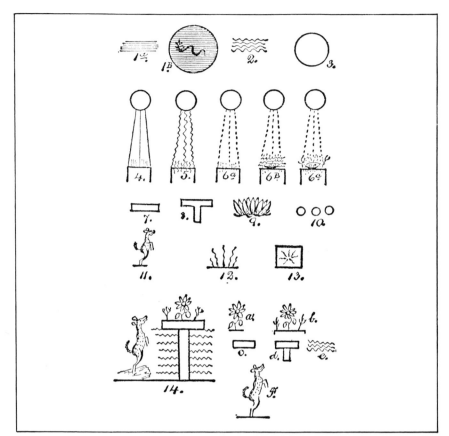

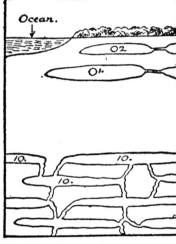

Left and below: Two of James Churchward's fascinating sketches illustrating his theory about Mu. The symbols are copies from the Naacal Tablets, and the diagram shows how rising gases destroyed the continent

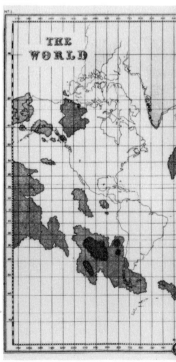

numerous other examples, and I should like to mention two more which fall within the scope of this book, Mu and Lyonesse. The better known is probably Mu, a continent said to have been larger than Atlantis itself and sited in the Central Pacific. Unlike Atlantis, Mu does not have a written tradition dating back to Greek times, and owes much of the interest it has attracted to one man, James Churchward, a world traveller and former member of the Bengal Lancers. It was Churchward who, in a series of books including *The Lost Continent of Mu* (1931), claimed to have deciphered two sets of ancient stone tablets, one set found in Mexico and the other owned by a priestly order in India, which told the story of the continent of Mu and its eventual destruction when gases trapped below the earth suddenly exploded some 12,000 years ago and caused the teeming civilization to sink below the waves.

According to Churchward, Mu was a luxurious continent measuring 6,000 by 3,000 miles; its sixty-four million inhabitants, known as Lemurians, possessed an advanced technology which not only gave them a life of comfort and ease but had provided them with anti-gravity devices with which they could actually fly. They were also responsible for sending out parties of colonists who, Churchward claimed, populated all the great land masses, including Atlantis, and it was some of these people who left behind the tablets containing a pictorial record of their history.

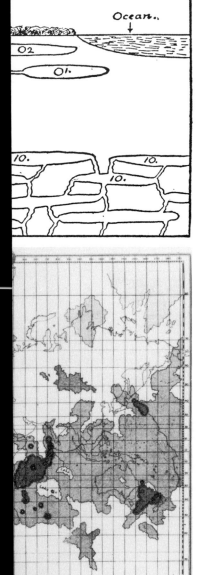

Bottom: The Theosophical
Society's map of Lemuria

The idea of this continent seems to have first developed in the nineteenth century when scientists began to note amazing similarities between forms of animal and plant life separated by thousands of miles of ocean. The name Lemuria was given to the land mass by Professor Philip Sclater, a zoologist and fellow of the Royal Society who declared, 'So certain, indeed, has the law been found to be of adjoining countries producing similar animals and plants, that the converse of this proposition is now generally accepted by naturalists . . . that if the animals and plants of two countries are alike, they must either now be, or recently have been, in geographical connection.'[35] Professor Sclater called the continent Lemuria after the Lemur and its relatives, whose habitat is limited to Africa, South India and Malaya, although in the Eocene Age they probably inhabited the entire northern hemisphere. He also suggested that the land mass had stretched from the Malay Archipelago across the south coast of Asia to Madagascar. Among the impressive list of Professor Sclater's supporters were the evolutionist Thomas Huxley and the German biologist Ernst Haeckel, who was the first to suggest that Mu was 'probably the cradle of the human race, which in all likelihood here first developed out of anthropoid apes'.[36] He believed that in Mu the Garden of Eden had at last been found.

Apart from Churchward's alleged Indian tablets – which no one else has seen – physical evidence about Mu is scanty, to say the least. Only one other source of material has subsequently been offered, by a Mr F. Bruce Russell, a retired psychologist from Los Angeles: in 1947 he announced that he had found a group of mummies eight to nine feet tall which were from the lost continent of Mu – the location was, though, somewhat prosaic: St George, Utah! (In connection with the Mu story, some other investigators have suggested that Mu was actually the remnant of a much larger and still earlier continent in the southern hemisphere which they called Gondwanaland, and which had once stretched three-quarters of the way round the world!)

The legend of the lost world of Lyonesse which is sited off the English coast is inextricably entwined with the stories of that great British hero King Arthur and his powerful magician Merlin. According to the tradition the area between Land's End and the Scilly Isles was once above water and was a place of prosperous communities and verdant fields. Then, in just one night, the land sank and the sea rushed in, engulfing landscape and people alike.

According to the historian Christopher Grey in *The Lost Land of Lyonesse* (1974), the legend says that this catastrophe was brought about by Merlin as revenge for the slaying of his friend and monarch Arthur by the traitor Mordred. Mr Grey writes: 'Mordred and his army were pursuing the fleeing forces of the dead king through Lethowsow, which was said to be the old name for Lyonesse, when he was suddenly confronted by Merlin. The magician did not speak but simply raised his arms. Thereupon the sky darkened, great red clouds rolled across the sky and the ground shook and with a mighty roar sank. Then the sea rolled in between pursuer and pursued, and Mordred and his men were drowned, even as Pharaoh and his army perished in the Red Sea.'

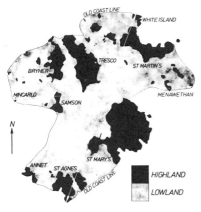

Although there is little material to support this legend, there is undeniable geological evidence to suggest that the Scilly Isles were once part of the Cornish mainland, but thousands of years ago – probably long before the time of Stone Age man. There are also a number of interesting old accounts about the land, two of which I should like to cite. One of these is actually the first written record we have, and is the work of the English chronicler William of Worcester. In his fifteenth-century work, the *Itinerary*, which was based on the now lost monastery libraries of the west, he made several references to Lyonesse, which, he said, consisted of 'woods and fields and 140 parochial churches, all now submerged, between the Mount and the Isles of Scilly'. A fuller report is provided by the Cornish antiquary Richard Carew in his *Survey of Cornwall* written 150 years later. 'And the encroaching sea hath ravined the whole country of Lioness, together with divers other parcels of no little circuit; and that such a Lioness there was, these proofs are yet remaining. The space between the Land's End and the Isles of Scilly, being about 30 miles, to this day retaineth that name in Cornish – Lethowsow – and carrieth continually an equal depth of 40–60 fathoms, a thing not usual in the sea's proper

Opposite above: Christopher Grey's map of Lyonesse

Opposite below: St Michael's Mount, Cornwall

Right: King Arthur's Round Table

Below: The Isles of Scilly

dominion. Save that midway there lieth a rock, which at low water reveals his head.'

Carew's report goes on with the unlikely story that 'fishermen casting their hooks thereabouts have drawn up pieces of doors and windows' (these were more likely to have come from shipwrecks around this notoriously dangerous coast), but adds interestingly, 'Moreover the ancient name of St. Michael's Mount was Cara Clowse in Cowse: in English "The Hoare Rocke in the Wood", which is now at every flood encompassed by the sea, and yet at some low ebbs, roots of mightie trees are descried in the sands about it.'

The antiquarian's report was, in fact, a major source of inspiration to the archaeologist O. G. S. Crawford when he conducted the first major enquiry into the legend in the Scilly Isles in 1926. He paid particular attention to reports of low spring tides revealing the sea bottom, where he personally observed tree-stumps and the remains of walls and actually picked up a number of flints. He concluded his report: 'There are good reasons for believing that the substance of the legend is true: that within prehistoric times there did actually exist land which is now covered by the sea.'[37]

Some modern archaeologists are now inclined to think that the answer to the mystery may well lie in the Cassiterides – the 'tin islands' referred to in Phoenician, Greek and Roman history, and said to have been located near Britain. The earliest reports refer to the islands as lying in the western sea 'beyond the countries of Spain and Portugal'; later they are described by Caius Strabo, a Greek geographer of the first century AD, as 'opposite to the west parts of Britain'.[38] It is argued that these islands could hardly have been confused with the great land mass of Cornwall, and that the scattering of small islands which make up the Scillies may once have formed part of a larger land mass rich in tin mines which provided the basis for trade with the early maritime nations. With the passing of time, the sea encroached upon the land – and there is plentiful evidence, for instance, of Roman occupation sites well below the present high-tide marks in the area – and what had once been the single island of Lyonesse became in time the modern Scilly Isles. Based on his research into and around this theory, Christopher Grey has drawn up the map reproduced here which indicates what he believes to be the extent of the original land mass. He is convinced that the evidence of the extensive tin mining which once attracted those European merchants is now beneath the sea, but points out that traces of mining can still be found in the Scillies. He feels that when the sea finally encroached upon the low-lying areas the people made themselves primitive boats and sailed off the island. 'Doubtless', says Mr Grey, 'some remained behind. They would have continued to work the shrinking surface of their island which, as the centuries passed and the sea level rose, was split up into several smaller islands until, by the first century AD, when Strabo lived, the memory of the island of Lyonesse could have deteriorated into a legend of a vast, lost land reaching to Cornwall and would instead have become the "tin islands".'[39] Could this be the final solution to the mystery of King Arthur's legendary island in the west?

An engraving of Plato

The Wonderful Island of Atlantis

An extract from Plato's *Timaeus* – the statement of the Egyptian priest to Solon about Atlantis, as narrated by Critias

MANY GREAT and wonderful deeds are recorded of your state [Athens] in our histories. But one of them exceeds all the rest in greatness and valour. For these histories tell of a mighty power which unprovoked made an expedition against the whole of Europe and Asia, and to which your city put an end. This power came forth out of the Atlantic Ocean, for in those days the Atlantic was navigable; and there was an island situated in front of the straits which are by you called the pillars of Heracles; the island was larger than Libya and Asia put together, and was the way to other islands, and from these you might pass to the whole of the opposite continent which surrounded the true ocean; for this sea which is within the Straits of Heracles [the Mediterranean] is only a harbour, having a narrow entrance, but that other is a real sea, and the land surrounding it on every side may be most truly called a boundless continent. Now in this island of Atlantis there was a great and wonderful empire which had rule over the whole island and several others, and over parts of the continent, and, furthermore, the men of Atlantis had subjected the parts of Libya within the columns of Heracles as far as Egypt, and of Europe as far as Tyrrhenia [Etruria in North Italy]. This vast power, gathered into one, endeavoured to subdue at a blow our country and yours and the whole of the region within the straits; and then, Solon, your country shone forth, in the excellence of her virtue and strength, among all mankind. She was pre-eminent in courage and military skill, and was the leader of the Hellenes. And when the rest fell off from her, being compelled to stand alone, after having undergone the very extremity of dangers, she defeated and triumphed over the invaders, and preserved from slavery those who were not yet subjugated, and generously liberated all the rest of us who dwelt within the pillars. But afterwards there occurred violent earthquakes and floods; and in a single day and night of misfortune all your warlike men in a body sank into the earth and the island of Atlantis in like manner disappeared in the depths of the sea. For which reason the sea in those parts is impassable and impenetrable, because there is a shoal of mud in the way; and this was caused by the subsidence of the island.

VI
PHANTOM ISLANDS

The spectacular island of Surtsey

THE RECENT widespread discussion about the strange area of the Atlantic Ocean known as the 'Bermuda Triangle' has focused public attention on the whole question of sea mysteries. Whether one accepts the argument that the triangular-shaped area bounded by Bermuda, Miami and the island of Puerto Rico possesses some inexplicable force that has been responsible for the disappearance of more than a hundred ships, aeroplanes and boats and with them over a thousand people, or whether the mystery is the result of confused research and wishful thinking – and both sides have marshalled considerable evidence for their respective points of view – the story is typical of sea enigmas. The reader probably scarcely needs reminding of all those tales of phantom ships like the *Flying Dutchman* and the *Mary Celeste*, the endless reports of sea monsters and the bizarre accounts of freak weather conditions unheard of on land. Nautical history is full of such items.

But one category which has been almost completely overlooked in this fascination with sea mysteries is that of the Phantom Islands: small land masses that have been reported by reliable mariners with great conviction and have then proved impossible to find again. Sometimes these islands have figured in old legends, being said to rise from the ocean deeps on one day and disappear the next. Others have been located, charted, even visited for a time, and then seemingly lost as mysteriously as they were found. For all those who love a good sea mystery these stories have an endless fascination which can be heightened by poring over maps and charts – both ancient and modern – of the areas where they are supposed to lie.

The legends of the Lost Elizabethan Islands of the North Atlantic are as fulsome as any, and just as hard to substantiate. This group is said to lie in the vicinity of Latitude 57° 35′ North and Longitude 26° to 27° West of Greenwich, and consists of several land masses of varying size. The larger islands have been named Frislanda, Icaria, Drogeo, Pondando, Neome and Busse. They are all located on the famous Zeno Chart of 1558 and mentioned in the works of several authorities, including Thomas Wright (1810–87), the English antiquarian who helped to found the Archaeological Association, and Justin Winsor (1831–97), the Boston historian and notable biographer of Columbus.

The most fully documented of the islands is Busse, which has been the centre of several remarkable events, the first of which gave it its name. The story began in 1578 when the intrepid maritime explorer Martin Frobisher set out on what was to be his last voyage of discovery to the far north-west. His fleet included fifteen ships, of which the important one in our story was the *Emanuel*, a busse, or small three-masted craft, weighing about seventy tons and captained by a man named Newton from Bridgwater in Somerset.

In Frobisher Bay the fleet ran into a violent storm, and in the confusion the *Emanuel* became separated from the rest. As the captain and crew battled against the elements, so the story goes, the look-out shouted that they were drifting too near land. So it was decided to ride out the storm in the lee of the island, and, the following day, land on it.

Next morning Captain Newton was amazed to find no reference to the island on his map. According to James Leecke, the Master of the ship, and the *Emanuel's* log book, the situation was about '25 leagues to the North West of Frieland' (probably Greenland).[40] The crew members who went on to the island found that although it had two good natural harbours the land was completely barren and the only living things to be seen were sea birds, including the occasional albatross. It was decided to name the strange place after the vessel which had brought the sailors there.

Sir Martin Frobisher – from the portrait in the Bodleian Library

Captain Newton reported his discovery when he returned to London, and subsequently several other mariners attempted to confirm the existence of Busse. In 1605 Captain James Hall failed to find it on an outward journey, but, a year later, saw a land mass through a driving snowstorm which he believed was the island. Three years later, the great English navigator Henry Hudson, making his ill-fated voyage in the *Discoverie* to Greenland (which nonetheless resulted in his name being given to the sea, strait and river which now bear it), sighted what he thought was Busse Island. However, as he was steering towards it, so the story goes, 'it seemingly sank into the waters, leaving no sign of its existence'.[41]

This report, perhaps more than any other, helped the island to become regarded as a phantom or myth: but it did not stop intrepid sailors looking for it. None, however, apparently succeeded, until 1635 when a Captain Fox reported that he had located it again, describing it as 'of considerable size, partly surrounded by ice and of queer appearance'.[42] He placed it at Latitude 57° 35' North and Longitude 26° to 27° West of Greenwich. The other members of the Lost Elizabethan Islands were close by, he added.

In 1671 Busse was spotted once more by a Captain Thomas Shepherd who had been fishing in Frobisher Bay. As a result of his account the island at last found a place on Seller's Chart, one of the most important of navigator's maps. With its existence apparently established, the island became a topic of intense interest among seamen and land dwellers alike. But when it reappeared on another map in 1745 – that of Van Keulen – seemingly as a result of a new sighting, it was completely different in shape from the Busse of Shepherd's version. The mystery deepened.

Thereafter each new sighting gave Busse a different shape, and in 1775 it apparently reverted to the tactic which had so surprised Henry Hudson: as it was approached it disappeared beneath the ocean waves.

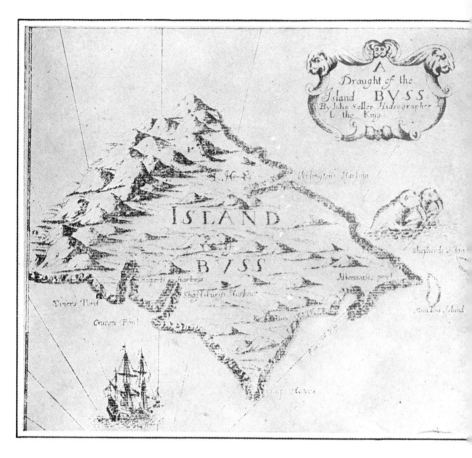

John Seller's map of the legendary island of Busse

Opposite above: The cartographer Toscanelli's fifteenth-century map, used by Columbus on his first voyage across the Atlantic, showing the island of Brasil (Bresail) near Ireland and St Brendan's Isle

Opposite below: The discovery of Graham's Island – an illustration from the 1895 edition of Jules Verne's *Captain Antifer*

Since this date neither Busse nor any of the other Elizabethan Islands has been seen again, although dozens of explorers have sought them out; the famous navigators Sir John Ross and Sir William Parry actually carried out soundings on their supposed sites, but with little success. The French author Jules Verne was fascinated by the story of the Elizabethan Islands and made partial use of it in his *Mysterious Island*. He also used the factual story of Graham's Island, which appeared in the Mediterranean, in his novel *Captain Antifer* (1895). This island, also known as Julia Island and Hotham's Island, suddenly erupted from the ocean on 28 June 1831 and a volcano in the centre 'burned with a continuous light'. The island was apparently covered with ashes and hot sand, but it was possible for people to land and walk around the perimeter. In December 1831 the island suddenly sank and disappeared as mysteriously as it had appeared. At the end of his story Verne could not help wondering whether Graham's Island might not appear again – 'then it may be possible to have another ending to these wonderful adventures of Captain Antifer!'

Another island which is said to rise and fall in the Atlantic Ocean lies beyond the Arran Isles and is referred to in several oral traditions in the south-west of Ireland. It is first recorded in the twelfth-century *Topographia Hibernica*, written by the Norman-Welsh historian and ecclesiastic Giraldus Cambrensis,

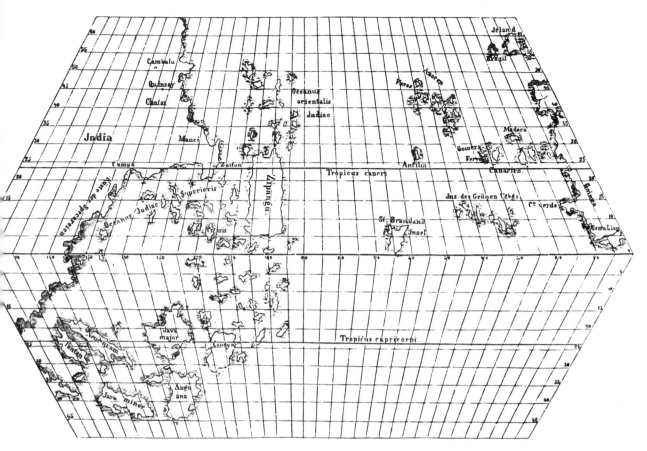

who made a special study of the 'history, people and marvels' of Ireland. He writes:

> Among the other islands is one newly formed, which they call the Phantom Isle, which had its origin in this manner. One calm day a large mass of earth rose to the surface of the sea, where no land had ever been seen before, to the great amazement of islanders who observed it. Some of them said that it was a whale, or other immense sea-monster; others, remarking that it continued motionless, said, 'No; it is land.' In order, therefore, to reduce their doubts to certainty, some picked young men of the island determined to approach nearer the spot in a boat. When, however, they came so near to it that they thought they should go on shore, the island sank in the water and entirely vanished from sight, The next day it re-appeared, and again mocked the same youths with the like delusion. At length, on their rowing towards it on the third day, they followed the advice of an older man and let fly an arrow, barbed with red-hot steel, against the island; and then landing, found it stationary and habitable.

St Brendan, the monk referred to in the chapter on the discovery of America, is said to have visited this island, and indeed to have spent seven Easters there. According to the tradition the island was originally named Bresail and was an earthly paradise until an outbreak of sin among its inhabitants caused it to sink beneath the waves; ever since, it has reappeared from time to time at sunset to warn sailors of approaching bad weather. (The position most often attributed to the island is now occupied by a shoal named 'Porcupine Bank'!)

There are also believed to be other phantom islands in this vicinity, including Flath-Innis, the Noble Isle, which again is only seen occasionally. It was once the home of an order of Druids who possessed miraculous powers and who apparently tried out a ritual of such potency that it caused the island to tremble and then submerge. Like Bresail, it only appears to presage trouble.

For over two hundred years, many maps showed an island designated as 'Brazil' lying a few hundred miles west of Southern Ireland. It was usually shown as circular, and received its most spectacular publicity in 1674 when a Captain Nisbet arrived in Scotland with some castaways he claimed to have rescued from Brazil. According to the men the island was in the control of a magician who had kept them under a spell in his castle, and the whole place was overrun by huge black rabbits! Despite many more authentic reports that Brazil simply did not exist, it was not until well into the nineteenth century that the mapmakers finally dropped it from their charts.

Another phantom associated with magic is said to lie not far from the island of Enhallow in the Orkneys. This was once the home of the great wizard Michael Scott, who had command of the Powers of Darkness and raised spirits and familiars to live with him and do his bidding. For generations it has been claimed that when the island rises from the waters a haunting music can be heard which lures people towards it. Those who cannot resist are doomed to go down with the island when it sinks again. To this day there are old people in the Orkneys who speak of having seen this island and heard the music that nearly enchanted them to their deaths.

The southern Atlantic and Pacific Oceans are just as rich in stories of phantoms – indeed, did not the Antarctic explorer Sir James Ross, the nephew of Sir John Ross, actually go so far as to call one land mass he charted off the coast of Victoria Island 'Doubtful Island'? (He was right to do so, in fact, for it turned out to be a huge iceberg!)

One such group of phantoms were the three Aurora Islands, supposedly lying to the south-east of the Falklands, which were so literally believed in at the beginning of the last century that, according to one commentator, 'their existence was as little doubted as that of Australia'.[43] Yet where are they today?

The islands were first discovered in 1762 by the ship *Aurora* which gave them their name. The captain and crew did not, however, attempt to land or chart the islands; nor did their second visitor, Captain Manuel de Oyarvido of the Royal Philippine Company in his ship *Princess*, who passed by in 1790. Captain de Oyarvido did, however, note their location carefully and this enabled a corvette of the same line, the *Atrevida*, under her captain, J. de Bustamente, to carry out an exact survey four years later.

Captain de Bustamente wrote in his report, 'We took all necessary observations and measured by chronometers the difference of longitude between these islands and the port of Soledad in the Maluineso. The islands are three; they are very nearly in the same meridian, the centre one is rather low, and

1

2

96

3

THE RE-DISCOVERY OF A 'LOST' ISLAND

Colonial Office Official Photographs from the Royal Research Ship, *Discovery II*.

Bouvet Island, in the far South Atlantic, was first discovered by a French naval officer, Pierre Bouvet, in 1739, but was afterwards 'lost' for years, and even modern charts have hitherto marked its position as 'doubtful'. The above photographs were taken from the royal research ship, *Discovery II*, during a voyage to the Antarctic. The island's exact position has since been charted recently by Vice-Admiral E. R. G. Evans—famous as 'Evans of the *Broke*'—now Commander-in-Chief of the Africa Station. He left Simonstown, the naval base near Cape Town, on February 15, for a 3000-mile patrol cruise in H.M. Sloop *Milford*. His primary object was definitely to locate Bouvet Island. He also intended to survey the southern whaling grounds and possibly touch the Antarctic Continent at a fresh point. When about 1000 miles out on her voyage, the sloop encountered heavy gales, which necessitated 'heaving-to', and at first it seemed necessary to return to Simonstown. Fortunately, however, the storms abated and the *Milford* eventually succeeded in reaching Bouvet Island, which was duly charted. Thus the first stage of the cruise was satisfactorily accomplished.

Illustrated London News, 3 March, 1934

1 THE 'MYSTERY' ISLE OF THE REMOTE SOUTH ATLANTIC RECENTLY CHARTED BY VICE-ADMIRAL E. R. G. EVANS: BOUVET ISLAND—A VIEW PREVIOUSLY TAKEN FROM THE RESEARCH SHIP, *DISCOVERY II*, SHOWING KAISER WILHELM PEAK.

2 ICEBERGS OFF CAPE NORWEGIA, IN BOUVET ISLAND: A PICTURESQUE HEADLAND OF THE LONG 'LOST' ATLANTIC ISLE NAMED AFTER THE FRENCH NAVAL OFFICER WHO FIRST SIGHTED IT IN 1739.

3 NO LONGER 'DOUBTFUL' ON THE CHARTS: BOUVET ISLAND—ANOTHER PHOTOGRAPH SHOWING CAPE VALDIVIA AND (ON RIGHT) THE ICEBERGS OFF CAPE NORWEGIA SEEN IN THE PHOTOGRAPH ABOVE.

the other two may be seen at nine leagues' distance.'[44]

The captain provided the following names and locations for the group: Northernmost or New Island, 52°37′ South, 47°43′ West; Centre or Low Island 53°2′ South, 47°55′ West; and Southernmost Island 53°15′, 47°57′ West. He said the islands were all cold and dark, exposed to freezing winds and in part covered with snow. The good man was certainly not over-enthusiastic about his surveying task and appears to have headed for home as soon as his data was complete. He was a dedicated seaman, nonetheless, and ensured that his 'discoveries' were included on the major maritime maps forthwith. They presented yet one more obstacle for ships and sailors battling round the dreaded Cape Horn.

In 1820, however, that remarkable explorer Captain James Weddell, who devoted his life to maritime affairs (giving his name to that icy waste the Weddell Sea) set out to chart the Auroras in still more detail: and was unable to find a single trace of them. Following Captain de Bustamente's figures exactly,

Captain James Weddell searching for the illusive Aurora Islands – an illustration from his book *Voyage Towards the South Pole* (1825)

Weddell sailed backwards and forwards across the longitude and latitude markings, allowing the fullest margin for errors, but had to conclude that the islands were phantoms. He wrote in his journal: 'Having thus diligently searched through the supposed situation of the Auroras, I concluded that the discoverers must have been misled by appearances; I therefore considered any further cruise to be an improvident waste of time; and to the gratification of my officers and men, directed our course to the Falkland Islands.'[45]

After the carefully considered verdict of such a man, one would have expected the story of the Auroras to die quickly – but not so. In the following ten years explorations were carried out by Johnson, Morrell and Biscoe, and although none could find anything, the tradition still survived – aided, no doubt, by the fact that once the cartographers had the islands on their maps they were most reluctant to remove them. Indeed, the Auroras remained on most maps until late in the nineteenth century.

As far as seamen were concerned, there was perhaps an unconscious reason for wanting the Auroras to exist, because of the legend that a Spanish galleon, the *San Telmo*, had been wrecked on their shores in 1819 bearing a fortune in gold and silver. It was this legend, plus the general mystery of the Auroras, that inspired Edgar Allan Poe to write his only full-length novel, *The Narrative of Arthur Gordon Pym*, in 1838.

'Sightings' of the islands still continued to be made by seemingly reliable witnesses. In December 1856, the *Helen Baird* noted in its log, 'At 4 a.m. the chief mate reported icebergs to leeward; going on deck, pronounced them to be the Auroras covered with snow.'[46] The crew of his ship actually reported seeing five islands, and on some Spanish maps of the period the group was shown as consisting of five islets.

However, the weight of evidence caused the group to be consigned to the category of myth, even though the occasional report still came in, like that of Captain B. H. Hatfield of the *Gladys* in June 1892: 'Lat. 52°55′ S., Long. 49°10′ W., land was reported on the lee quarter, it appeared like a long island with two hummocks rising up from the top, dividing the island into thirds, which would appear like three islands. At 8 a.m. discovered another island distance about ten miles . . . It looked as if there might be passage between this island and the long island.'[47]

And so the mystery has remained. Maritime opinion seems to favour the idea that the Auroras were in fact a smaller group of rocks in this vicinity charted as the Shag Rocks, but even this solution does not completely answer all the questions.

Not far to the north of the alleged site of the Auroras lies another phantom island, 'Isla Grande', which was reported in 1675 by Antonio de la Roche, the discoverer of South Georgia. The island lay on the forty-fifth parallel and was described by de la Roche as 'very large and pleasant, having a good harbour towards the eastward'.[48]

Unfortunately the Spaniard did not pinpoint his island carefully enough, and while it found a place on contemporary maps the general consensus of opinion

The Phantom 'Isla Grande' reported by Antonio de la Roche in 1675, an illustration which appeared in Captain Weddell's *Voyage Towards the South Pole*

grew against its actuality after several expeditions failed to find anything. It is now believed that the 'Isla Grande' may have been nothing more than a projecting point on the South American mainland.

To the east of the Auroras, and about 1,500 miles south-west of the Cape of Good Hope, lies the island of Bouvet, a kind of phantom island in reverse; for this spot of land – probably the most isolated place in the world, there being nothing within a radius of 1,000 miles of it – was for years thought to be a myth and yet has subsequently been proved real. It was discovered in 1729 by the French naval officer, Pierre Bouvet, who must have come across it in all that vastness of ocean by the most amazing good luck. He called the place 'Cap de la Circoncision' believing because it was so shrouded in fog that it was a promontory of the long-sought-after Southern Continent. (It was not until Cook's second voyage in 1772–5 that this continent, Antarctica, was found much further south.)

Because later explorers were searching for what they imagined to be the tip of a huge land mass, the 'Cap de la Circoncision' failed to show up in general surveys of the area and was consequently dismissed as a myth. Then in 1808 an expedition from London decided to concentrate on finding an island, rather than a promontory, and established that the land mass was in fact a tiny island about five miles in diameter, of which the 'Cap de la Circoncision' was the north-west extremity. Nonetheless, scepticism about Bouvet remained for half a century, especially among maritime people: as the island was frequently enveloped in ice it could easily be written off as a huge table iceberg. But today Bouvet Island is an established though lonely fact: the phantom island that became a reality.

Moving north to an almost equal distance beyond the forty-fifth parallel we come across the mysterious Saxemberg Island with its strange history. This South Atlantic island was first noted in 1670 by a Dutch navigator named Lindeman, who gave its location as Latitude 30°40′ South and Longitude 19°30′ West, a position about six hundred miles north-west from that other highly remote spot, Tristan da Cunha. The island was said to be verdant and lush with a high mountain rising from its centre.

Several unsuccessful expeditions appear to have been mounted to find Saxemberg, including one by James Horsburgh, later of the East India Company, who worked on the basis that the latitude designated was wrong, and

Captain Matthew Flinders, who in 1801 did find birds and turtles in the designated area – an indication of land – but no positive sighting of the island. Both returned home disappointed.

In 1804, however, the American Captain Galloway in his ship *Fanny* reported coming across Saxemberg. He said he had had the island in view for four hours and could clearly distinguish the tall peak, but set its longitude two degrees further eastward, a considerable discrepancy. Twelve years later the British ship *True Briton* reported spending six hours in sight of the island. Its commander Captain Head confirmed the peak seen by both Lindeman and Galloway, with the longitude just as the latter had stated.

Despite the exactitude of all these reports, Saxemberg Island has never been reliably sighted again, despite extensive searches and soundings carried out in the area. The notorious American sealer Captain Benjamin Morrell Jr did claim an extraordinary encounter with it in his *Narrative of Four Voyages to the South Sea* published in 1832: 'On Saturday, August 23 1828 we were roused by the cheering cry from the masthead of "Land ho, land ho, about six points off the starboard bow." We now had the wind from west-by-south, which permitted us to haul up for it; but after running in that direction about four hours, at the rate of eight miles an hour, our tantalising land took a sudden start, and rose about ten degrees above the horizon. Convinced that we could never come up to it in the ordinary course of navigation, we backed and stood to the northward.'

Whatever one makes of this story, it has to be born in mind that Morrell was known in his day as 'the biggest liar in the Pacific'. Even with the passage of time, though, it has not been possible to dismiss this strange island completely: some authorities have suggested that all the sailors saw was strange cloud formations on the horizon, others that Lindeman may have mistakenly believed he saw an island, and that those who followed him, similarly wanting to see something, fell victims to 'expectant attention' – the well-known condition of wishful thinking. A few, though, still cling to the idea that Saxemberg Island waits, lonely in the vastness of the Southern Atlantic, for a final claimant.

There is good enough reason, too, for not finally closing the file on another island seemingly lost in the waters away to the south-west of Cape Horn – 'Dougherty Island'.

The story of this mystery began in 1800 when an American whaler, Captain Swain, sighted an island 'covered with snow and abounding with sea dogs [seals], and fowl'.[49] He named it after himself and charted its position as Latitude 59° South, Longitude 90° West. A few years later another American seaman, Captain Richard Macy, sighted the island and confirmed the geographical features mentioned by his predecessor with the additional information that it was 'four or five miles in extent' and the water around it 'was much coloured and thick with rock-weed'.[50]

After these two reports, several other American ships undertook searches of the area, but were unable to find 'Swain's Island': consequently it was soon being considered a myth. Then, in 1841, Captain Dougherty, the captain of a British whaler, the *James Stewart*, seemed to lay all the doubts to rest when he entered in his ship's log: 'May 29, 1841, at 2 a.m. saw land ahead, luffed and cleared it. It appeared an island 5 or 6 miles in length, running N.E. and S.W., with a high round bluff on the N.E. end, with low land to S.W.: between N.E. and S.W. ends there appeared a valley covered with ice and snow; we passed it within a quarter of a mile, going ten knots: Latitude 59°20'S., Longitude 120°20'W.: the position of latitude and longitude may differ a few miles by reason of not having had proper observations for several preceding and following days.'[51]

In 1859 a report confirming this statement was made by Captain Keates of the *Louise*, who described the island as 'round and dark-coloured, about 80 feet high'.[52] Thereafter the island – now renamed 'Dougherty Island' – found a place on Admiralty maps and other important charts.

There was still much argument about its existence, however, and in 1909 a New Zealand sealer, Captain White, who knew the area well, felt constrained to come to its defence. 'Any doubt as to its existence', he wrote, 'is all nonsense. We have passed round it and lassoed cub seals there. The latitude can be relied on; longitude fairly good, but may be a few miles farther east. As for some people saying it does not exist, I would bet all the tea in China it does.'[53]

Just as firmly, however, other mariners have denied its existence after sailing the vicinity. Both the *Carnegie* and the *Nimrod* of Shackleton's first Antarctic expedition and Scott with the *Discovery* ran over the area but could find no trace. And so the argument has raged to the present day. 'Dougherty Island' has its supporters, who have periodically tried to arrange for new exploration, while its detractors believe the various sightings can be explained as having been of huge icebergs – for flat-topped bergs rising several hundred feet from the surface and five or six miles in length have been recorded in these waters from time to time.

There are, of course, other phantom islands to be found on the maps and charts of several oceans: a great many are the result of confused cartography, or the belief, in times gone by, in stories of lands which were nothing more than pure romance. Some, without the slightest basis in reality, were even put in by mapmakers to flatter their sponsors; the trouble came when later cartographers took them for real!

For the reader who is interested there are miniature 'phantom islands' that can be seen at a number of accessible places from time to time. At Derwentwater, in the English Lake District, for instance, an island rises up for a few weeks sometimes in the summer, and is substantial enough for people to land on. A similar specimen surfaces in Lake Orion in America, but has received little attention because it presents no danger to shipping. Another well-known example appears on Lake Victoria in Australia. All these floating islands are caused by marsh gas forming in layers of peat and debris on the lake floor and causing them to rise up when the water temperature is appropriate.

Opposite above: Derwentwater in the Lake District where an island sometimes rises into view during the summer months

Opposite below: Lake Victoria, where another 'floating island' surfaces from time to time

Hierro, one of the Canary Islands, where the inhabitants watched the rise and fall of a phantom island just off their coast in 1967

Perhaps, though, the most extraordinary view of a phantom island in recent times was that enjoyed by the inhabitants of Hierro, one of the Canary Islands, on 26 April 1967. The story is fully attested and exhaustively documented in newspapers and official reports.

For three centuries and more there have been continuing reports of a phantom island – named by some St Brendan's Isle, by others seen as a fragment of the lost Atlantis – which regularly rises from the sea in this vicinity. Indeed, in the eighteenth century accounts of its appearance were so frequent and definite that the local authorities several times organized expeditions to take possession of the land!

On the April morning in question, scores of the people of Hierro were about their daily tasks when suddenly a huge land mass began to rise from the sea towards the north-west. As they stood open-mouthed in amazement, the phantom lifted itself fully into view. The crowds of watchers soon swelled from hundreds into thousands as the island remained in view for over an hour, afterwards slowly sinking back into the ocean depths.

The amazed population were in no doubt as to what they had seen – Hierro lies at the eastern extremity of the archipelago and there is, therefore, no island in the neighbourhood that could have caused a mirage, the Cape Verde Islands, 900 miles to the south-west, being the nearest. The day was also not a particularly hot one. To everyone who had seen it, this was the proof that the phantom island of their seas did exist. And should you go there, and talk to the people as I have done, you will find their belief quite unshakable.

In his recent book *The Mysterious Unknown* (1969) Robert Charroux, the leading French expert on the supernatural, has speculated further on whether this phantom island might in some way be connected with the legend of Atlantis. 'It is extremely curious to note', he writes, 'that the island appears in the North Atlantic shallows – at the very spot where Plato and other traditionalists placed Poseidonis, the capital of Atlantis.'

A fanciful illustration of a captured sea monster

A Phantom Island Sighted!

An extract from the log of the *Atrevida* kept by Captain J. de Bustamente,
quoted in *Oddities* by Commander Rupert T. Gould, London 1928

"IN THE year 1794, on the 20th of January at 5 and a half p.m., we perceived to the northward, at a great distance a dark lump, which appeared to all of us like an iceberg. Notwithstanding, we bore away for it under a press of sail; and when we were near it, we saw distinctly a great mountain in the form of a tent, divided vertically into two parts; the eastern extremity *white*, and the western very *dark*; on which latter side was a belt of snow; and we noticed some breaks in the dark streak.

"We passed within one mile of the island, coasting it on the western side; and from that point, it presented us the view of a sharp rock, trending from north to south. The southern part, constantly exposed to the freezing winds from that quarter, was covered with snow; and, falling perpendicularly on the north-west side, with winds much more temperate and moist, the land was there perfectly discoverable.

"At daylight, we saw another island at a great distance, also covered with snow, but not so high as the former one. At 6h. it might be distant ten miles, to the N. by E., and the first island was seen to the S.E., distant about eight miles. At 9h. we lost sight of it (the second island); and although the wind freshened from the N.W. we went round it without result, because, the clouds not having dissipated, we could not observe the latitude at noon. We nevertheless waited, and at one o'clock had an altitude, and another at three o'clock. . . .

"The wind was now at S.W., and we hauled to the southward, seeking in higher latitudes more favourable winds to get to the westward and make the coast of Patagonia.

"On the 24th, at midday, we were in 55° 28′ latitude S.; and as we did not meet better winds, but rougher seas and more intense colds it was resolved to lessen the latitude, in search of more favourable weather. We stood to the northward, on the port tack, with all sail; and on the 26th, at evening, discovered to the E. 1/4 N.E. a white lump, which at first appeared to us an iceberg; but its immobility soon convinced us that it was an island. It is a large rock, making in sharp pinnacles, but formed like a saddle-hill. The N.E. was covered with snow, but the southern part, being perpendicular, would not retain it. At a mile from this last point, there extended several breaking reefs, terminating in small islands. We coasted along this great rock at a regular distance, and sounded frequently, without finding bottom.

"We all agreed that these were the Auroras, but were much puzzled that so few of the circumstances agreed with what had been reported of them. . ."

De Pygmæis Gruntlandiæ, &

M SEP.

MONS · HVIT · SARCH

e Huitſark.

VII

THE SECOND RACE

A war-like small man shown as an inhabitant of America before the arrival of Columbus and the European explorers. An eighteenth-century Scandinavian engraving by Hvitsaerk which appeared in *The Discovery of North America Twenty Years Before Columbus* by Sofus Larsen, published in London in 1925

DID MANKIND once share the earth with a race of tiny beings who as we developed and progressed withdrew into seclusion, to become in time nothing more than the subject of legends and myths? Could remnants of this 'Second Race' be the fairies and leprechauns of folk tales, the wild men and wee folk of superstition? For while such creatures have a central place in our mythology, it is now being argued that they are not the inventions of fantasy but real beings.

The theory has already found numerous supporters in both the scientific and lay fields, all subscribing in effect to the opinion of an anonymous contributor to *Antiquary* who wrote in 1926, 'Then God created Man, and afterwards he created the Second Man, doomed to live his primitive life forever in secret.' In a nutshell, investigators believe that many of the recurring stories can be explained by this theory. Writing on these legends in his book *Strange Creatures from Time and Space* (1975) John A. Keel says, 'Numerous Indian tribes in western United States and Canada have stories about "little men" who come to specific lakes and rivers for water year after year; these places have been avoided by the Indians and regarded as sacred. The Irish have always told us of "little men" in tight-fitting green or brown costumes who frequent lakes and rivers on the old sod. While most of us tend to dismiss the leprechaun lore of Ireland as folk tales and myth, there are a number of impressive and well-documented books relating the numerous appearances of these tiny, elusive beings. The leprechauns are supposed to live underground, too, and woe to anyone who tries to find their hiding places.'

One of the best known proponents of the idea of a Second Race is probably Arthur Machen (1863–1947), the Welsh macabre story writer and journalist, who, though he enjoyed scant financial reward or critical acclaim during his lifetime, is now regarded as one of the most important figures in the realm of supernatural literature. Machen was born and grew up in the mysterious region of Caerleon where King Arthur is thought to have held his famous court and spent much of his childhood wandering the hillsides and caves of the area. He became an expert in the lore of the supernatural, and was particularly drawn to stories of the fairies and goblins who were said to dwell in profusion in the area.

As an adult he moved to London to work as a journalist, but never lost his interest in the occult, and indeed joined a number of the leading mystical societies to further his enquiries. It was here that he began his study on the

Above: A Swabian woodcut dated *c.* 1480 which some claim shows a sleeping pedlar being robbed by tiny men

origins of the 'little people'.

Machen came to the conclusion that these tiny folk were not wholly imaginary, but were the descendants of the prehistoric people who had inhabited Europe before the arrival of the Celts from the north. He added weight to his theory by drawing on evidence collected by anthropologists that a race of small Mongoloid people who were workers in flint had flourished during the Neolithic, or polished stone, Age. They were known variously as Turanians, Picts and Mediterraneans, and the relics of their time unearthed by scientific research showed them to have reached a comparatively high stage of primitive culture by the beginning of the Bronze Age.

It was at this time that the Celts moved south and either destroyed or enslaved the little people already living there. The Celts were themselves later ousted by the Teutonic tribes. From the time of this second invasion, stories began to emerge that not all the diminutive folk had been slaughtered – some had been able to hide themselves away in caverns and holes, emerging only at night to steal their food and carry out occasional reprisals on those who had oppressed them by stealing small animals and even sleeping children. These captures, it was said, were used in sacrificial rites.

Machen expressed his feeling about the secret race most succinctly: 'They are horribly evil,' he wrote, 'and they are something more – or something less – than human.'[54] It was easy to see how the stories of these little marauders had become, with the passage of time, turned into the legends of fairies, goblins, leprechauns and so on. He believed there was ample evidence of their existence to be found in several areas of Europe, including his own Wales, Ireland, Scotland, central France and the Basque provinces of Spain; even America and Central Asia could not be excluded.

Below left: An alleged photograph of leprechauns

Below: Boris Porshnev, the Russian investigator of the 'secret people'

Machen, of course, expounded his theory in a primarily fictional form – perhaps his best story utilizing the theme being *The Shining Pyramid* – but others have been more direct, such as Professor Boris Porshnev, the director of the Modern History Department of the U.S.S.R. Academy in Moscow. Professor Porshnev's theory is a variation on that of Machen, for he believes that mankind can go backwards as well as forwards – that there is devolution as well as evolution. Both the human race and the secret people of legend (Professor Porshnev includes fairies and leprechauns as well as larger mysteries such as the Abominable Snowman in his theory), he claims, have descended from common ancestors. But whereas the human race developed ultimately into the rulers of the world, our one-time brothers have slipped back towards animal existence. According to his theory, the split came in the Neanderthal stage, which may have lasted from 400,000 to 50,000 years ago. Neanderthals, he says, were unquestionably human beings: 'they could cook, make simple tools, they probably wore clothes and spoke some sort of language'.[55]

Professor Porshnev believes that the modern survivors of this race, apart from their hairy covering and large heads, are very much like us. However, they are now devolved to the point where they have lost their skills and probably have no language. With the spread of humanity across the globe

Right: An illustration of
anthropoids from
Hoppus's *Anthropomorpha*,
published in 1760

Below: A German woodcut
dated 1477 showing a
hunter chasing two small
people

they have been obliged to retreat into the remote areas of the world: mountains, forests and deserts. The Professor claims that the Neanderthals' hatred for human beings makes them difficult to find: the few people living in areas where modern Neanderthals sometimes appear have been regarding them as hallucinations or wishful thinking based on old superstitions. That might even be as well, for he believes they are cannibals and this is the reason why none of their corpses have been found.

The Professor thinks the strongest link in his theory is the Abominable Snowman, personifying the half-way stage between monkey and man, and he is convinced he could prove it by capturing one. He also feels that expeditions to the snowbound Himalayas to find the creature will fail – because it does not live in the snow, merely crossing it (thereby leaving its footprints) on the way from one remote valley to another.

Evidence of the tiny people of the kind that Machen and Porshnev speak about has also been found in the form of structures and artifacts which seem to have been made by diminutive hands. Archaeologists have, for instance, long been puzzled by the maze of tiny tunnels and stairways found in the pre-Inca ruins of Sachuaman and other South American cities which date from the dawn of time, for these tunnels are so narrow that children find them difficult to crawl along and their doorways could only be easily used by dwarfs and midgets. There is no sign of those who might have used them; only miles of narrow tunnels cut through solid rock and deeply worn by tiny feet. In the United States, also, at Exeter in New Hampshire, there is an ancient complex of tunnels and tiny chambers built long before the Indians. According to John A. Keel, who has investigated the site and studied the legends, the local Indians firmly believe that the 'little men' constructed the place. Just as puzzling are the artifacts that have been found at various other places around the world, including beautifully worked little ivory pieces from Shemya in the Aleutian Islands, and the so-called pigmy flints, perfect arrowheads scarcely half an inch long but undoubtedly shaped by human hands.

Those who have investigated the whole fascinating idea of a Second Race have also drawn attention to the races of comparatively small people that can be found around the world: the Bushmen of Africa, for instance, who average four feet in height, and the Australian Aborigines, who are all less than five feet tall, and many much tinier than that. Aside from these, there are those two well-known categories of little people that can be found just about everywhere: dwarfs, who have normal-size trunks and heads but short arms and legs, and midgets, who are generally well-formed but much smaller than normal people. In both groupings there have been famous figures. Aesop, the author of the *Fables*, and Attila the Hun were both dwarfs under three and a half feet tall, while Tom Thumb the midget made himself and his exhibitor P. T. Barnum a fortune.

Perhaps more closely allied to the Second Race theory are the numerous stories throughout history of creatures called 'woodhouses', 'wodehouses',

An ape or a wild woman? A disputed engraving from Bontius's *Historia Naturalis* of 1658

Wudewasa or simply 'wild men'. One has only to glance through ancient books and illuminated manuscripts to come across illustrations of small men completely covered by hair or fur, often walking on all fours, and looking extremely fierce.

As Ivan T. Sanderson, the American investigator of the unexplained, has written of these pictures in his essay 'Wudewasa', 'Because of the overwhelming number of illustrations known to exist of these wild men, because of the diverse historical periods and wide geographical distribution of the artistic depictions of them, it seems quite certain that they once walked this earth and perhaps not so long ago.'[56]

In comparing the illustrations one finds careful attention given to showing both the hands and feet of the wild men as being hairless: a point made to demonstrate that the artists were not confusing them with the various primates. Nor were they depicting men dressed up in costumes for festivals. This consistent factor can be seen in such diverse drawings as the *Hunguressu* of the Mongolians, the *Gin Sung* or 'Bear Man' of the Chinese and the *Dzu-Teh* of the Nepalis. Commentators have also noticed how these different wild men have, almost without exception, been armed with wooden clubs of a very similar nature and protected themselves with crude shields of a kind found in the earliest cave paintings such as those in Spain at the *Cuevas del Civil* near Albocacer Castellón. All the men in the picture are small of stature and have short legs and long arms. They have comparatively large heads with shortish hair and fringe beards under their chins. The brow-ridges are pronounced and 'beetle-like', the nose is large, the mouth wide and full and the naked face invariably black and shiny.

'From detailed studies of these mediaeval depictions,' Ivan Sanderson says, 'combined with those of some earlier depictions on pottery, and later illustrations in early natural histories, we are forced to the conclusion that a type or types of primitive, fully-furred or haired human beings with long arms, beetling brows, dark skins, and possessed only of wooden implements, were spread throughout central and northern Europe until the 14th Century, though they seem to have died out in the Mediterranean area during the middle Roman times.'

Tracing their history he goes on:

> It has long been taught that the Neanderthalers disappeared from Europe at the end of the last ice advance, and it is implied, at the hand of Cro-Magnon man. However, Cro-Magnon man appeared rather abruptly on the extreme western fringe of the continent, and it would seem that the other peoples in the late Paleolithic and Mesolithic stages of advance also spread into the Mediterranean from the west, ending with the appearance of the Iberians.
>
> Even today there remain considerable areas in northern Sweden and the Caucasus that have not been explored. Settlement followed by civilisation spread northwards into Europe from the Mediterranean basin but took several thousand years to reach the ultimate peripheries of the continent. During this period post-glacial conditions continued undisturbed in many places until the Fourteenth Century.

Left: An illustration of a Second Race man from Edison Marshall's novel *Ogden's Strange Story* (1934)
Above: An eighteenth-century German engraving of a wild man carrying off a child
Below: A 'Wudewasa' – an illustration from Ivan T. Sanderson's study of these furry men (1964)

Neanderthalers and other primitive humanoids or sub-men were not exterminated overnight by Cro-Magnon nor any other race of modern men. In some areas they appear to have been absorbed rather than exterminated. In other areas they just removed themselves, probably back to the forests. Not being tribalised, the Neanderthalers undoubtedly did not fight unless attacked and cornered individually or in family groups.

For these reasons, Mr Sanderson concludes, 'it may be inferred that the Neanderthalers disappeared from Europe very gradually over a long period: and that some of them remained in central Europe until Mediaeval times, and some may still survive in the two extreme limits of that continent – in northern Sweden and the Caucasus'.[57]

Only recently Mr Sanderson and the Russian Professor Porshnev have been publishing a growing amount of evidence of the existence of such wild men in the mountains of northern Iran, spreading through the Pamirs to the whole of the Mongolian upland areas of eastern Eurasia. Their very latest findings indicate that the species may even have spread into the forested areas of eastern Siberia.

Other places that have been cited as home for the little men are Africa and Australia. In eastern Africa particularly it is said there exists a race of tiny brown-skinned, red-haired people known as *agogwe*. An encounter with them is mentioned by the English historian and traveller S. V. Cook:

> Fifteen miles east of Embu Station there rises from the Emberre plains the lofty hills of Dwa Ngombe, nearly 6,000 feet high. They are inhabited, the Embu natives say, by buffalo and a race of little red men who are very jealous of their mountain rights. Old Salim, the interpreter at Embu. tells me with great dramatic effect of how he and some natives once climbed to near the top when suddenly an icy cold wind blew and they were pelted with showers of small stones by some unseen adversaries. Happening to look up in a pause in their hasty retreat, he assures me that he saw scores of little red men hurling pebbles and waving defiance from the craggy heights. To this day even the most intrepid honey hunters will not venture into the hills.[58]

I have also heard tales of a similar race of little 'red men' in the Mississippi Delta area of America who are said to be about the size of a ten-year-old child, can climb like monkeys and live in the heart of the bayous. In Australia, according to an article published in *Nature* in 1972, it was reported that the last remnants of a tiny species of man believed to have vanished 200,000 years ago were still living in the Kow Swamp region. There are also numerous other reports of a similiar kind from countries outside the scope of this book.

Perhaps the most intriguing element of all in the mystery of the little people – or the Second Race, if you care for the title more – was the discovery, not so long ago, of a tiny mummified man in a cave. Not a cave in some isolated spot in Europe, but in Wyoming in the heart of America!

The story began in October 1932 when two gold prospectors were working in a gulch at the base of the Pedro Mountains about sixty miles west of Casper

Above: A rare photograph of the mysterious 'little man of Wyoming' from *Exploring the Unknown* magazine, May 1965, and (*right*) the mummified body, found in Central America, of what is believed to be a Second Race man.

in Wyoming. Suddenly they came across what looked like an indication of gold on one of the gulch walls and decided to blast into the stone with dynamite.

Setting their charges, the men withdrew and waited for the explosion. After the smoke and debris had cleared, they returned to find they had exposed a cave about four feet wide by four feet high and fifteen feet deep. Peering inside they were amazed to see the tiny figure of a man sitting cross-armed and cross-legged on a ledge. He was dark bronze in colour, very wrinkled, and no more than fourteen inches high!

The men had never seen anything like the little mummy and decided to take it back to Casper – where not one of the thousands, laymen and scientists alike, who subsequently came to see the creature had either. Some anthropologists thought it was all a hoax – how, after all, could a body be found in solid rock? Yet when an X-ray was taken, a skull, spine, ribcage and bones, almost exactly like those of a normal man, were clearly discernible. Closer study established that the creature weighed about twelve ounces, had a full set of teeth and was probably about sixty-five years old when he died.

Yet when did he die? And, more important, who was he? These were the questions that baffled everyone. First, it was the turn of the experts to have their say. The Wyoming State Historical Society were in no doubt that the creature was human, and one of their number, Dr Henry Fairfield, a noted scientist, named it 'Hesperopithicus' after a form of anthropoid which supposedly roamed the North American continent during the middle of the Pliocene Period. Anthropologists from Harvard were satisfied that the little man was genuine and shared the opinion of Dr Henry Shapiro of the American Museum of Natural History, who had X-rayed the tiny body and said it was 'of an extremely great age, historically speaking, and of a type and stature quite unknown to us'.[59] A theory that the creature might be a mummified infant was investigated by the Boston Museum Egyptian Department, who declared emphatically that while the method of its preservation seemed to match that of the Egyptian Pharaohs, there was no question of its having been anything other than fully grown when death had occurred. Although there was a great deal of agreement as to the little man's authenticity, none of the experts seemed to be able to take the matter much further.

It was some of the old local residents who put the investigators on to the most intriguing idea of all. They said the little man was just one of a race of tiny people who had once populated the region. Naturally, the suggestion was at first greeted with hoots of laughter; then those of a more open mind began to make further enquiries and check old records and found that there might well be something in the story.

Coral E. Lorenzen, who has recorded details of the story in her book *The Shadow of the Unknown* (1970), says that although the Indians have traditionally always been held as the first inhabitants of America (arriving originally from Asia over a land bridge that once existed across the Bering Straits), a race of tiny people may already have been there. She writes,

The history of the area in which the little mummy was found goes back far beyond that of the Arapaho and Shoshoni, who inhabited that part of Wyoming in the relatively recent past. Petroglyphs [engraved pictures] found on the cliffs of Dinwoody Canyon were believed, by Vincenzo Petrillo, the eminent archaeologist, to have been placed there thousands of years ago. The petroglyphs in the area show evidence of having been added to or having other glyphs superimposed over them many times. Indian legends hold that 'little people' lived in the obscure canyons and carried on wars against them. Several writers have visited or lived with the Shoshoni and Arapaho Indians, from whom they learned the legends of the little men – their way of life, the food they ate, the clothing they wore and the poisoned arrows with which they fought.

Miss Lorenzen cites several stories told by Indians about encounters with these people, including the account of twelve Shoshoni braves who had just killed a number of buffalo and were skinning the carcasses when they suddenly found themselves surrounded by a band of little men who screamed and threatened them. One of the buffalo that the Indians had killed was white, and as the party decided to beat a retreat from the screaming horde, a brave grabbed this particular skin and threw it round his shoulders. Immediately the little men backed off, screaming with fear. The braves stopped, puzzled,

A remarkable photograph of a little man taken in the thirties. It has been alleged that the small man is a flying saucer crewman who was taken from the remains of a saucer that crashed near Mexico City

Opposite: Engravings of the famous 'Peter the Wild Boy' who was exhibited in Europe during the early years of the last century

117

and then realized it was the white skin that had changed the mood of the little men: the pelt obviously had some significance for them, and, armed with it, the Indians obviously had nothing to fear from their tiny adversaries. Miss Lorenzen does not believe the little men were just confined to Wyoming, and says that there is a legend that the Pueblo tribe of the Stone Lions in New Mexico were attacked by pygmies who slaughtered many of their number and drove the rest away. She adds, further, that in 1950 she saw the mummified remains of a number of little people in glass cases in the Carlsbad Caverns in New Mexico. 'This might indicate,' she goes on, 'that some time perhaps thousands or millions of years ago, and possibly even more recently – there were not only giants in the earth, but pygmies also, and not the sort of pygmies with whom we are acquainted. Where did they come from? Do they still exist, perhaps carefully concealing themselves from civilisation? Perhaps we will never know. . . .'

Perhaps we will never know – but then perhaps we may: for each discovery like the little man of Wyoming helps push our knowledge a little further forward, and who is to say we shall not learn still more surprising things about the Second Race in the future? It is important that we should continue to think and debate, as Frank Edwards has emphasized in his book *Stranger than Science* (1959): 'Scientists from far and near have examined this tiny fellow and have gone away amazed. He is unlike anything they ever saw before. Sitting there on the shelf in Casper, visible, disturbing evidence that science may have overlooked him and his kind much too long.'

A photograph of Arthur Machen taken in 1910

The Terrifying Little People
An extract from *The Shining Pyramid* by Arthur Machen, London 1936

"I SHUT myself in my room, and endeavoured to dismiss all prejudice from my mind, and I went over everything *de novo*, assuming for theory's sake that the disappearance of Annie Trevor had some connection with the flint signs and the eyes on the wall. This assumption did not lead me very far, and I was on the point of giving the whole problem up in despair, when a possible significance of the Bowl struck me. As you know there is a 'Devil's Punch-bowl' in Surrey, and I saw that the symbol might refer to some feature in the country. Putting the two extremes together, I determined to look for the Bowl near the path which the lost girl had taken, and you know how I found it. I interpreted the sign by what I knew, and read the first, the Army, thus: 'there is to be a gathering or assembly at the Bowl in a fortnight (that is the Half moon) to see the Pyramid, or to build the Pyramid.' The eyes, drawn one by one, day by day, evidently checked off the days, and I knew that there would be fourteen and no more. Thus far the way seemed pretty plain; I would not trouble myself to inquire as to the nature of the assembly, or as to who was to assemble in the loneliest and most dreaded place among these lonely hills. In Ireland or China or the West of America the question would have been easily answered; a muster of the disaffected, the meeting of a secret society, vigilantes summoned to report: the thing would be simplicity itself; but in this quiet corner of England, inhabited by quiet folks, no such suppositions were possible for a moment. But I knew that I should have an opportunity of seeing and watching the assembly, and I did not care to perplex myself with hopeless research; and in place of reasoning a wild fancy entered into judgment: I remembered what people had said about Annie Trevor's disappearance, that she had been 'taken by the fairies.' I tell you, Vaughan, I am a sane man as you are, my brain is not, I trust, mere vacant space to let to any wild improbability, and I tried my best to thrust the fantasy away. And the hint came of the old name of fairies, 'the little people,' and the very probable belief that they represent a tradition of the prehistoric Turanian inhabitants of the country, who were cave dwellers: and then I realized with a shock that I was looking for a being under four feet in height, accustomed to live in darkness, possessing stone instruments, and familiar with the Mongolian-cast of features! I say this, Vaughan, that I should be ashamed to hint at such visionary stuff to you, if it were not for that which you saw with your very eyes last night, and I say that I might doubt the evidence of my senses, if they were not confirmed by yours. But you and I cannot look each other in the face and pretend delusion; as you lay on the turf beside me I felt your flesh shrink and quiver, and I saw your eyes in the light of the flame. And so I tell you without any shame what was in my mind last night as we went through the wood and climbed the hill, and lay hidden beneath the rock.

"I think I need say very little more. You know we were quite helpless, even if we had foreseen what was to come. Ah, the particular place where these signs were displayed? Yes, that is a curious question. But this house is, so far as I can judge, in a pretty central situation amongst the hills; and possibly, who can say yes or no, that queer, old limestone pillar by your garden wall was a place of meeting before the Celt set foot in Britain. But there is one thing I must add: I don't regret our inability to rescue the wretched girl. You saw the appearance of those things that gathered thick and writhed in the Bowl; you may be sure that what lay bound in the midst of them was no longer fit for earth."

VIII
ABOMINABLE CREATURES

An artist's impression of a group of Abominable Snowmen

WHILE the general public's interest in the idea of a Second Race is still rather restricted – in the main due to the paucity of open discussion of the topic – the concern with strange land creatures roaming the backwoods of civilization has reached almost cult proportions. The Abominable Snowman is by far the best known of all such creatures which live on the borderland of fantasy and reality, and whose acceptance as fact is strongly advocated by one group of experts and just as strongly denounced by their opponents. Creatures that are the subject of old legends, baffling reports and disputed sightings – even blurred photographs – they are to be found throughout the world in remote locations and are becoming the centre of a whole new area of enquiry. Like all the topics in this book, the Abominable Creatures are once again a puzzling mixture of fact and sheer conjecture.

The Abominable Snowman is reputedly a half-man, half-beast whose primary habitat is India and Tibet, although recent study claims that he is just one of a strain of such creatures to be found in China, Russia and across the Bering Straits in Canada and America. Although in the vicinity of the Himalayas, where he has been most sighted, the Snowman has apparently been a tradition for centuries, it was not until 1887 that he found mention on a wider scale in a book, *Among the Himalayas*, by a major in the Medical Corps of the British Indian Army, Lawrence Waddell. Waddell recounted that while he was in the province of Sikkim he came across the footprints of a creature, obviously barefoot, which had shown the most amazing agility in its passage across treacherous snow and rocks. 'These', he wrote, 'were alleged to be the trail of the hairy, wild men who are believed to live amongst the eternal snow.' Intrigued though he undoubtedly was, the major did not investigate further, but he had quite unintentionally sparked off the interest in the creature which has grown to such enormous proportions today.

The popular name for the creature, Abominable Snowman, did not emerge until 1920 when the first British Mount Everest expedition under the leadership of Colonel C. K. Howard-Bury was attempting to climb the Tibetan or northern face. Reaching about 17,000 feet on the Lhapka-La Pass, the party were startled to see through their binoculars a number of dark figures holding themselves upright and moving about on a snowfield far above them. When, later, they reached the snowfield they found a large number of huge footprints which Colonel Howard-Bury described as being 'three times the

The Tibetan Lama in this photograph, taken by Professor C. von Fürer-Haimdorf at Pangboche in 1954, is allegedly wearing the scalp of a yeti on his head

size of those of normal humans'.[60] The Sherpas in the group immediately became very excited at the discovery and identified the tracks as belonging to creatures to which they gave a variety of names, including *mehteh kangmi*, *mirks*, *sogpa* and *yeti*. When, later, the Colonel decided to send back news of his find to India, he chose the Sherpa words *mehteh kangmi* – meaning 'man creature, snow creature' – to describe what he had seen, but somewhere along the line the first word became garbled as *metoh*. Although puzzled, the recipients were sure the message must have considerable importance and, therefore, asked a man with enormous local knowledge, Mr Henry Newton, a columnist on the *Calcutta Statesman*, to translate it for them. He too was probably baffled, but this did not deter him from giving an immediate translation, equating the mysterious word with the Tibetan *metch*, a term of disgust, and announcing that *metoh kangmi* meant 'Abominable Snowman'. At a stroke, the world, and the newspapers in particular, had a new sensation. As a matter of interest, Colonel Howard-Bury, whose message played such a crucial role in the story, never really believed in a half-human creature: he felt the footprints were those of 'a very large stray, grey wolf'.[61]

A year after the Colonel's expedition, the second British Everest party, under the leadership of General C. G. Bruce, actually questioned the Head Lama of the Rongbuk Monastery about the Snowmen and were told that five of them lived in a nearby valley. Unfortunately the General did not follow up the lead. Then, a few years later, two English explorers, Hugh Knight and N. A. Tombazi of the Royal Geographical Society, claimed, independently of each other, to have actually seen the yeti, describing it as resembling a big man with a barrel chest and overlong arms, and having yellow skin, mongoloid features and blond hair. Knight said that the creature he saw was actually carrying a crude bow and arrow.

Three of the most important photographs of yeti tracks. *Above:* Eric Shipton's picture showing the size of the Snowman's footprint compared with that of the boot of a climber, and (*far right*) a line of tracks taken during the same expedition in 1951. *Right:* Magazine cutting showing the first ever photograph taken of a yeti footprint.

FOR COMPARISON WITH THE IMPRESSION OF A BEAR'S FOOT: AN "ABOMINABLE SNOWMAN'S" FOOTPRINT PHOTOGRAPHED BY THE LATE MR. FRANK SMYTHE IN THE HIMALAYAS IN 1937.
(*From "The Illustrated London News" of November 13, 1937.*)

The legend was not to receive its major impetus until sixteen years later, when actual photographs of the Snowman's footprints were secured, but in the interim reports of more footprints came from several expeditions including those of the American Ronald Kaulback in 1936 and Eric Shipton in 1937. It was at this juncture that the first 'explanations' of the prints began to be offered, and the fact was commented upon that the footmarks were almost always found in a straight line: something seemingly impossible for a large creature to achieve. It was said that the prints were nothing more than the sun-enlarged tracks of bears, giant pandas, monkeys or similar creatures, and that the sightings were tricks of the snow and sunlight. But these arguments hardly held up in the face of the report in 1949 of a large group of Sherpas who were gathered for a religious festival and saw the creature at a distance of *eight feet*!

The first photographs allegedly of the creature's footmarks were obtained in 1937 by Mr Frank Smythe on an expedition to Everest, and these received worldwide publicity in newspapers and journals of all kinds. It was suggested, however, by experts at the Natural History Museum that the marks might well have been those of a Himalayan species of brown bear that is known to travel above the snowline. At this time, too, a purely human origin for the stories of the Abominable Snowman was suggested. Apparently in Tibet it was the custom with convicted murderers, instead of executing or imprisoning them, to turn them loose to fend for themselves for the rest of their lives. These 'dirty outcasts' took to dwelling in caves and feeding off small animals and vegetation while their appearance became progressively more animal-like and their hair grew and their clothes rotted to pieces. Such men, according to one opinion, naturally had to avoid normal humanity and when spotted might well seem to superstitious and fearful minds to be less than human.

More impressive photographs still were those taken by Eric Shipton on the Menlung Glacier in 1951. Shipton, an Everest veteran of some years, had seen yeti tracks several times previously, but never as clear as on this occasion. He also reported the description of a Snowman which had been given to him by a Sherpa porter who claimed to have been within twenty-five yards of one of the creatures: 'The Sherpa said it was half-man, half-beast, about 5 ft 6 inches tall, covered with reddish brown hair, but with a hairless face.'[62] Despite the most intensive tests by London scientists it proved impossible to link Eric Shipton's photographs and the moulds he took of the footprints with any specific animal known in the Himalayas. The mystery was now wide open, as Ivan T. Sanderson has written in his study *Abominable Snowman: Legend Come to Life* (1961):

> The whole affair was, until Eric Shipton published his photographs, really nothing more than a news-gimmick, though the press had to tread warily with the reports made by prominent persons and especially the mountaineers engaged in the attack of Everest, which had official backing. The scientific world had not been quite so circumspect. At the outset, it denounced the whole thing as, first a fraud, and then a case of mistaken identity, and it stuck to this

story: and it still in large part sticks to it today, even to the extent of deliberately ridiculing such men as Shipton and Kaulback. But after their completely unsuccessful attempt to set Shipton's 1951 findings at nought, which backfired with considerable public impact, a sort of revolution began within the ranks of science.

This 'revolution' took the form of properly supervised investigations into the whole subject, and drew in scientists, anthropologists and zoologists from London, Switzerland, France and even Russia. There was also a newspaper-sponsored expedition to the Himalayas in 1954 to look for the yeti which, although not very successful, brought into focus one point which previously everyone had overlooked – that because the snowfields of the Himalayas were barren of any foodstuffs, these creatures must live elsewhere, probably in the dense forests on the lower slopes. It was an important point which subsequently changed yeti-hunting radically. Also on to the scene at this time came the benevolent and energetic American Tom Slick, who not only sponsored extensive exploration of the abode of the Snowman – going along himself, too – but initiated the school of thought that these creatures might not just be restricted to the Everest area. Slick believed they were large, ape-like things with pointed heads who lived off small field animals and roots and herbs. Simultaneously, too, the Soviet Academy of Sciences initiated an enquiry into the matter, sending expeditions to the major points in Asia where such creatures had been reported. Ivan Sanderson writes, 'There were four in number and were put into the field in 1958 – one to the Caucasus where a creature named the "Wind Man" had been rumoured for centuries; one to the north face of the Everest bloc; one to the Mongolian regions; and one to the Pamir, which, for certain odd reasons, they considered to be the breeding ground of the Abominable Snowmen.'[63]

As a result of their enquiries, the Russians were able to state emphatically that they believed the creatures were primitive Hominids (i.e. men) rather than Pongids (apes), and that various forms of them were to be found widely spread across the globe. Scientists everywhere were forced to sit up and take note at such startling news.

A Swiss investigator, Professor C. von Furer-Haimendorf, took another giant step towards dispelling any remaining doubts when he published photographs of an actual yeti-hide which he had inspected in the Himalayas. Writing of one of the photographs he said, 'Among the masks and ritual objects kept in a small Buddhist temple at Pangboche village there is a headdress believed to consist of the scalp of a yeti. It is made of strong hide, with sparse, bristly hair of brownish colour. Although there is reason to believe that the skin is, in fact, that of a yeti, it is probably not a "scalp" but a piece of hide from another part of the body, moulded into its present shape while still fresh and pliable.' The Professor added a further comment based on his research that 'Most Sherpas have seen a yeti at some time or other, and wall-paintings in monasteries and temples depict two types of them – one resembling a bear and one resembling a large monkey. It is generally known that there

Above: Three drawings showing the skull of an Abominable Snowman as reconstructed by Russian scientists (*top*), a Snowman sleeping, drawn by Professor Khaklov (*centre*), an ancient Mongolian mask (*bottom left*), and another drawing by Russian scientists of a yeti's face. These drawings are taken from Ivan T. Sanderson's *Abominable Snowman: Legend Come to Life*, published in Philadelphia in 196

Above right and right:
Yeti country – *Illustrated London News* photographs of the Imja Khola valley with Mount Everest in the background and (*right*) the Buddhist temple at Pangboche, where a yeti-hide is believed to be

The Abominable Snowman has become a popular figure, as these examples indicate. *Right:* Five postage stamps issued by the Government of Bhutan in 1966 depicting various impressions of the yeti. *Opposite:* A comic strip covering the main elements of the yeti legend, from *Marvel Comics*, 1975

are two such types, and that in hard winters they may come into the valleys and prey on the Sherpas' potato stores, or even on cattle.'[64]

Sir Edmund Hillary, the conqueror of Everest, also went in search of the yeti, and saw a number of the alleged scalps of the creatures. However, he came to the conclusion that the skins belonged to the rare Tibetan blue bear. Talking to the natives, he learned that there were not just two types of Snowman, but three. The first was called the 'clutch', a sandy-and-black-haired creature, about eight feet tall, with vegetarian tastes and only unfriendly when annoyed. The second, the 'mitch', was about four and a half feet tall, had a high, pointed head and was reported to be very dangerous. The third member of the trio, the 'thelma', was said to live only in forests. Sir Edmund was also shown what the Sherpas claimed were authentic yeti footprints, but he believed they were actually 'clusters' of pawprints made by a fox running very quickly. The end result of the Hillary expedition, as far as the Snowman was concerned, was that its leader disagreed with the other experts who believed that there was something in the stories. He said he could find no one who had ever seen the creature – nor was he satisfied with any of the evidence that was shown to him.

Despite the verdict of such an eminent man, evidence about the yeti has continued to pour in. In July 1973 there was a report that a young Sherpa girl had been attacked and knocked unconscious by an Abominable Snowman in the Khoner area near Everest. The creature, which killed five of the yaks which the girl was minding, was described by her as being 'four to five feet tall with thick black hair below the waist and brownish hair above'. It had long nails

WHEN THE WINTER SNOWS COVER THE EARTH, CHILDREN DELIGHT IN SHAPING THAT COLD WHITE STUFF INTO SNOWMEN. THE SNOWMEN OF TIBET, HOWEVER, ARE NOT MADE FROM SNOW. THEY ARE FLESH AND BLOOD, AND **QUITE DEADLY!**

THE ABOMINABLE SNOWMAN

In 1913, in the Himilayas, a small child was kidnapped from a village by a creature described as having a black, ape-like face and covered with long silvery-yellow hair.

BARON Weirwulf's LIBRARY

Hunters tracked the beast, which they called a YETI, and after a fierce struggle managed to wound it.

EDITOR-GEORGE WILDMAN
WRITER-NICOLA CUTI
ARTIST-NEWTON

D-6007

For months the YETI was kept captive at Patang, in Sinkiang Province, until it finally became ill and died. Years later more reports came in of many similar creatures.

In Katmandu, Nepal, Dr. Norman Dyrenfurth discovered the snowman's lair. Through footprints he calculated that the snowmen are of two species — one the size of a child, and the other, fully eight feet tall!

129

on thick fingers and 'sometimes walked on all fours and sometimes on its two feet'.[65] (This, in fact, is just the latest in a long line of stories from native sources of yetis attacking people, perhaps the best known being the kidnapping of a child by a creature with a black, ape-like face and long silvery-yellow hair at Patong in 1913.) Later that same month, a team of British zoologists exploring the high forested valleys of the Himalayas reported back that there was 'overwhelming evidence for the creature's existence'. They, however, were inclined to the view that it might be descended from the giant ape *Gigantopithecus*, and said that one of their tents was visited by an animal 'which left tracks that are not referable to any known animal'.[66] The team concluded that the yeti merely uses the high mountain passes to travel from one valley to another, and this is the reason why it has been seen more often by mountaineers than by anyone else.

The suggestion that Abominable Creatures like the Snowman might be found on a world-wide scale has caused some experts to try and link the yeti with another mysterious creature, the Sasquatch, or Bigfoot, which has been regularly reported on the North American continent. Ivan Sanderson, the American zoologist, explorer and author, has been in the forefront of these ranks, and has written several books discussing the reports of half-human creatures which have come in from all over the globe. He believes there are three similar but distinct breeds of Snowman of varying sizes and ranging from those human enough to engage in contact with local tribesmen to others so dangerous that they can kill a man with ease. He has even speculated that forerunners of present Abominable Snowman might have existed as far back as Old Testament times, and are actually mentioned in the Bible; he quotes Genesis 6: 4: 'There were giants in the earth in those days; and also after that, when the sons of God came in unto the daughters of men, and they bore children to them, the same became mighty men which were of old, men of renown.'

In terms of widespread public interest and speculation the North American Bigfoot creature is of a more recent date than the Abominable Snowman, but like its Himalayan cousin it has been known in Indian tradition from the earliest times. The word 'Sasquatch' is a distillation of several Indian names given to the hairy giant – *Seeahtik, Wauk-Wauk, Te Sami'etl Soquwiam, Wendigo* and *Saskahevis* – and first became commonly used by the Chehalis Indians of Fraser Valley in British Columbia, the area where the largest number of sightings has occurred.

The earliest known 'references' to the Sasquatch are found on the carved totem poles and masks of the coast Indians of British Columbia: a fact that helped dispel early scepticism that the whole matter was a hoax. On these items are to be found depictions of ferocious-looking wild men and women – the latter with large, pendulous breasts, a feature often remarked upon in modern sightings. Similar semi-humans are a part of Indian lore from British Columbia right into northern California, each one enjoying a variety of different names. To the Indians, though, there was nothing very mythical

Right: A frame from the famous Bigfoot film taken by Roger Patterson in Bluff Creek in 1967

Below: René Dahinden, Bigfoot hunter, with a wood carving of the creature

about the creature: it existed as part of their world, in sparsely settled and heavily timbered areas, but it was not something to be interfered with. The attitude of modern North American man has been quite different.

An important early account of a brush with a Bigfoot is contained in one of the books by the American President Theodore Roosevelt, who, apart from his political career, was a great hunter and zoologist. In his *The Wilderness Hunter* (1893) he recounts a story from the mid-1800s of two trappers in the Salmon River district whose camp was attacked one night by a 'great body . . . with a strong wild beast odour'. One of the men grabbed his rifle and drove the creature off with gunfire. The following morning, the men found strange footmarks around their tent, and later in the day thought the creature must still be in the vicinity because they heard 'branches crackle as it moved about, and several times it uttered a harsh, grating, long-drawn moan, a peculiarly sinister sound'. Although both trappers were tough, hardy men used to the worst that nature might inflict on them, they could not cope with the unknown, and grabbed their remaining traps and fled.

A still more remarkable incident occurred in 1884 when the only recorded instance of the capture of a Sasquatch took place near the town of Yale in the Fraser Canyon of British Columbia. The story was reported in the *Victoria Colonist* of 4 July and described how the creature had been seen apparently lying asleep beside the railway line by the engineer of a train. The man had applied the brakes and the sound of the stopping train had awakened the creature, which jumped up and ran off. The engineer and several others on the train then decided to give chase, and finally cornered their strange prey, rendering it unconscious by throwing a rock at its head. 'Jacko' – as the creature was later named – was quickly tied up and transported to Yale, where an eye-witness described him as 'something of a gorilla type standing about four feet seven inches in height and weighing 127 pounds'. He had long, black hair and 'resembles a human being with one exception, his entire body, excepting his hands and feet, is covered with glossy hair about one inch long'. 'Jacko' was apparently fed on berries and fresh milk but raw meat was withheld 'as the doctor thinks it would have a tendency to make him savage'. The *Colonist* report ended by asking whether 'Jacko' belonged to 'a species hitherto unknown in this part of the continent', but gave no hints as to his fate. Subsequent enquiry has failed to establish whether the creature was examined by any experts or whether the story that he died while being carted off to become an exhibit in a sideshow is true. It remains one of the greatest enigmas in the Bigfoot Saga.

Reports of other sightings continued to trickle in to newspapers on an ever-widening scale throughout the end of the last century and the beginning of this – the furthest from British Columbia being the account of a 'wild man' spotted by a group of hunters in Greene County, Arkansas. (In his exhaustively researched book *On the Track of the Sasquatch* (1968) journalist and leading Bigfoot expert John Green has estimated that the range of tracks reported during the last seventy-five years extends over an area more than a thousand miles in length and half a million square miles in area!)

It was to be in the United States, in fact, that the Bigfoot broke into the world headlines with two sensational appearances in 1958 and 1967 at the logging community of Bluff Creek in heavily-forested Humboldt County, northern California. The first of these happened in August 1958 when a bull-dozer operator named Jerry Crew found a number of large, naked footprints, human in shape, implanted in soft soil. Measuring the prints, Crew was amazed to find they were sixteen inches long, with the stride between each varying from forty-five to sixty inches – well over twice his own. At first his colleagues in the construction crew thought it was a hoax – but then when further footprints turned up on the site, and a number of heavy objects such as a fifty-five-gallon fuel drum were moved about at night, attitudes began to change. Said Crew, 'Those loggers could look at those prints and conclude that something bloody big and unusual had made them, but their minds couldn't, or wouldn't, take the final step and imagine just what it is.'[67] He himself went ahead and made plaster casts of the prints which he showed to the press – and soon the story of the creature roaming the woods of northern California was front page news across America. Any doubts that lingered among the workers of Bluff Creek were dispelled a little later when a party of men set out to try and trace the creature. As they drove along a deserted road their headlights suddenly picked up a giant figure that seemed to be human, or at least humanoid. It appeared to be both ape and man, or something in between, covered with brown hair or fur. Although they stopped the car and gave chase on foot, the men soon lost the creature. Their dogs, however, continued with the chase, and were soon all lost in the night. A few days later, the story goes, the dogs were found dead – each one looking like a 'sack of shattered bones'. Tom Slick, the philanthropist who had organized an expedi-tion to search for the Abominable Snowman, also financed a search for Bigfoot in the Bluff Creek area in 1959, which, although much time and money was expended, failed to unearth any new information.

If this episode may be said to have inspired the American interest in the Bigfoot, the film which was subsequently taken in the same vicinity of one of these creatures actually walking through a forest glade certainly made it a topic of worldwide appeal. On 20 October 1967 a former rodeo cowboy named Roger Patterson and his half-Indian companion Bob Gimlin were stalking the same area where Jerry Crew had made his first sighting when one of the creatures suddenly crossed their path, about ninety feet ahead of them. Patterson grabbed his movie camera and shot twenty-four feet of 16 mm colour film as the creature ambled across a ridge of timber and sand skirting dense forest. Patterson and Gimlin said that what they saw was a giant female with pendulous breasts, weighing about 350 pounds, and standing seven feet high. During the time they observed her she had looked round once before vanishing into impenetrable bush. Both men added that even from the distance where they stood, the pungent aroma given off by the creature nearly made them sick. Checking over the spot where the Bigfoot had walked,

Right: A map of the areas in Canada and America where the Bigfoot, or traces of it, has been seen

Below: Roger Patterson (*right*) and Bob Gimlin examine casts of the footprints of the Sasquatch that they saw and filmed

Patterson found a trail of huge footprints which were subsequently made into plaster casts.

Once Roger Patterson's film had been developed it became the subject of intense study by anthropologists, zoologists and film-makers. All three groups came to the conclusion that the film was not a fake and that it very likely did show the fabled Bigfoot. The official view was succinctly put by Dr Clifford Carl, director of the British Columbia Museum, who wrote in February 1968, 'Scientists and laymen who have studied the Sasquatch film and other evidence are faced with two improbabilities. If the tracks, sightings and photographic evidence are not real the Sasquatch is a hoax of colossal magnitude. If the evidence is real, the second improbability, that a pre-historic man-type mammal has been with us without leaving concrete evidence (teeth, bones, etc.) is staggering to the scientific world.'[68]

Since the Patterson film was taken, the arguments have continued to rage about Bigfoot and the reported sightings of it over the whole area of North America. Newspaper and magazine articles have proliferated, books have been published by the dozen, and one extraordinary story after another presented by the media. (Perhaps the most bizarre of all was the claim of a one-time logger, Albert Ostman, of Fort Langley, British Columbia, that he was kidnapped by a male Sasquatch and held captive for a week before escaping – with the help of a box of snuff. He kept the Sasquatch occupied with this while he ran. Ostman said that he had been taken for stud purposes, suggesting that the old male who grabbed him wanted him as a mate for his daughter! Interestingly, this story was actually related to Queen Elizabeth II when she was told about the local legend of the Sasquatch during her visit to British Columbia in 1959!)

Among the origins that have been suggested for the creatures is the idea that they are the remnants of a race who lived on the American continents ages ago. In dealing with this theory in his book *Sasquatch* (1973) Don Hunter says, 'Perhaps the "lost tribe" theory is a fanciful one which orthodox science would consider at least flimsy. But should it be found to be valid, the occasion would not be the first on which the halls of science have rung with the sound of surprise.' Even the sober *Wall Street Journal* has more than once investigated the phenomenon, and it put the current situation into focus when a reporter commented in August 1972, 'Bigfoot (Sasquatch) has emerged as a leading character in the world of the unexplained, ranking with the Himalayas' Abominable Snowman and the Loch Ness Monster in Scotland. Indeed, according to the growing number of believers, it's much more likely that Bigfoot does exist than it is that his mysterious counterparts elsewhere are real. To the believers, he's a living, breathing subhuman primate whose intelligence and instincts have allowed him to elude capture to date.'

Because of the international interest in the Abominable Snowman and the Sasquatch, information has also begun to be built up about other Abominable Creatures in many and various locations. Among those which reports indicate are similar in build and appearance are the *Nandi* and *Ngoloko* of Africa; the

Ban Manas, Bangjakri and Rakshasa of India; the Trolak Ape-Man and Orang Pendek of Malaya; and the Beruang Rambai of Sarawak. A much fuller list of these creatures and their names with particular reference to other countries such as South America, China and Russia is to be found in the index of Odette Tchernine's book *The Yeti*. Recently Miss Tchernine wrote an article in the journal *Oryx* (December 1974) on the likelihood of these creatures being a worldwide phenomenon. She says: 'Sightings, generally of a very dark, half-human, half-ape like figure and footprints have been reported from various points. But the yeti-snowman-sasquatch problem will only be solved if all knowledge is pooled and ways and means decided internationally for exploring the relevant places, quietly, simply and without too much modern equipment.'

In the end, as Edward D. Hoch wrote in his syndicated article, 'Something in the Snow' which appeared in the June 1974 issue of *True* magazine, any speculation of Snowman probabilities 'must centre around something very close to human life'. He goes on:

> In view of this, it is interesting to note that east Asia – the general area of the Himalayas – has yielded a great deal of evidence over the years toward investigation of the so-called 'missing link' between apes and man. Prehistoric skulls and bones uncovered in Java, China and elsewhere tend to prove that the area was an early home for such ape-like men. If several types of primitive humans existed in Asia centuries ago, it is not impossible that one has survived in small numbers, undetected by the men of science. The Abominable Snowman may be neither abominable nor a man of the snows. But it is something more than an ape or a bear that has been making those strange tracks in the mountains for all these years, something more that has been seen by travellers and natives in several parts of the world. Perhaps all we can surely say is that *something* waits up there.

The frozen ape-like creature found in the Bering Straits, from a photographic impression made in 1969

We cannot close this section without mentioning the strange hairy ape-like creature discovered frozen in a block of ice in the Bering Straits and subsequently exhibited in fairgrounds all over America. Although the creature was somewhat bizarrely described as 'possibly a mediaeval man left over from the Ice Age' it attracted tremendous interest among the crowds who flocked to see it – and the experts, as the *Sunday Times* reported in September 1969: 'The "creature" provided anthropologists with one of the most intriguing questions they had faced in years – was it a hoax, a freak, or was it, as the respected Belgian zoologist, Dr Bernard Heuvelmans, who first examined it suggested, a form of human being believed to have been extinct since prehistoric times? The Smithsonian Institute in Washington was interested. So was the Federal Bureau of Investigation, because the creature had two large bullet-holes in it. . .' According to the man exhibiting the creature, it belonged to a rich and eccentric Californian who refused to release any details about how it had come into his possession. Then, early in 1970, the owner reclaimed his strange frozen creature, and, rejecting all personal approaches, left only a few eye-witness reports and some artists' sketches as evidence of a most tantalizing mystery.

Chinese sketch of the yeti

Face to Face with an Abominable Snowman

Peter Byrne, Deputy Leader of the 1957 Slick-Johnson Yeti Expedition to Nepal, quoted in *Abominable Snowman: Legend Come to Life* by Ivan T. Sanderson, New York 1961

THE FIRST sighting was made by a Sherpa villager who said he was hunting edible frogs by the river at night with a torch hung on a bamboo pole. Moving upstream about 300 yards from Gerald's camp the man came upon a wet footprint on a rock. As he swung his torch low to examine it he saw a snowman squatting on a boulder across the stream, 20 yards away. The Sherpa was terrified, for tales of the Yeti in these mountain villages are full of accounts of the creature's strength and habit of killing and mutilating men. He shouted in fright. The beast slowly stood on two feet and lumbered unhurriedly upstream into the darkness.

The following night Gerald's Sherpa guide Da Tempa, a veteran Himalayan tracker from Darjeeling, went out with the villager at midnight, the note relates. While Gerald remarked it was "sporting" of the villager to venture out again, he noticed the fellow was trembling with fear and kept behind Da Tempa as they left the camp. After more than an hour of scouting up and down the Choyang River banks, Da Tempa and his companion were making their way back to Russell's camp when Da Tempa saw movement ahead on the trail. He thought it was probably leaves of a bush rustling, but shone his flashlight at the spot.

There, not more than 10 yards away, stood a small ape-like creature, the Snowman! The Snowman advanced deliberately toward the light, and Da Tempa turned and ran. Next morning Gerald said he found four very clear footprints in the gravel trail, which he has photographed. From questioning Da Tempa and the villager these facts emerged about our elusive quarry:

He is about 4 feet 6 inches high, with hunched shoulders and a very pointed head which slopes back sharply from his forehead. He is covered with thick reddish gray hair. His footprints are about 4 inches long. The villager was shown our pictures of bear, orang utan, chimpanzee, gorilla and prehistoric man. He unhesitatingly pointed to the gorilla picture as being most like the creature he saw, but he emphasized the head was more pointed.

IX
MONSTERS OF THE DEEP

An artist's impression of a sea monster seen by a
Frenchman, M. Renard, in the Atlantic Ocean
in August 1881 – an illustration from *The Great
Sea Serpent* by A. C. Dudemans, London 1892

S TRANGE, puzzling creatures which
may be remnants from the very earliest times are not confined to the land,
as the story of the Loch Ness Monster – to name but one – clearly demon-
strates. In a number of countries there are lakes and stretches of inland water,
as well as locations around the coast, which have been claimed as the homes
of mysterious water monsters.

Perhaps the one enigma which typifies this whole area of legend more than
any other is the aforementioned Loch Ness Monster, said to be a large secretive
'beastie' and 'probably the rarest and least-known of all living creatures',
according to one of its many biographers, Lt. Commander Rupert Gould, in
his book *The Loch Ness Monster and Others* (1934). Like its half-cousins on land,
'Nessie' is the subject of many stories, several photographed sightings, and
endless controversy between its supporters and opponents. Modern descriptions of it are often as fantastic as those found in Scottish folklore.

Loch Ness is actually three long, deep lochs, backing for twenty-two miles
through rugged mountains from the town of Inverness. At its widest point
it is barely two miles across. It has long been thought to be bottomless, and
although several times soundings have been taken, establishing its deepest
point successively at 754 feet, 820 feet and, most recently (1969), 975 feet,
scientists believe it may be deeper still. The loch is indisputably the largest
freshwater body in the British Isles and (at the present estimate) the third
deepest in Europe. For centuries it was a remote and lonely place, which
probably accounts for the legend of its formation. According to folklore the
area was once a green and fertile valley containing a magic well on which the
local residents depended for their water. An ancient prophecy said that the
well had to be kept covered with a stone slab when it was not in use or else
the waters would overflow and flood the valley. The inevitable happened,
it is said, when a woman was suddenly interrupted in the course of drawing
water by the frightened cries of her child who was playing nearby, and she
ran off without replacing the slab. The legend also relates that when the water
from the well filled the glen it released the monster which had lived in its
depths for untold generations. The more reliable evidence of geographical
study says that the loch is actually a sinistral wrench fault which probably
occurred more than 300 million years ago and was filled by a combination
of melting ice and sea water. What remains indisputable, however, is that
Loch Ness is clearly long enough to be the natural habitat for a creature the

An aerial photograph of Loch Ness from the Fort Augustus end

size of a whale and deep enough for it to be seen on only the rarest occasions.

Although there were apparently stories that the loch had been the home of a 'water horse' or Kelpie from time immemorial, the first recorded story of the monster dates from about AD 565 and concerns St Columba, the man who brought Christianity to Scotland. On his arrival at Loch Ness, it is said, the missionary was shown the body of a ferryman who had been attacked and killed by a monster living in the lake. Apparently not frightened, and needing to cross somewhat urgently, St Columba ordered one of his men to swim across the loch to the other side, where the ferryman's boat was still beached. What happened as the man struck out across the water is recorded in *The Life of St Columba* (*c.* 700) by the Irish monk, St. Adamnan: 'Now the monster was lying hidden on the bottom and seeing the water disturbed by the man who was crossing, emerged and moved towards him with his mouth open. Then the Blessed man looked on, while all who were there, the heathen as well as the brethren, were stricken with very great terror; and with his hand raised he formed the sign of the cross, and in the name of God commanded the fierce monster, saying, "Thou shalt go no further nor touch the man; go back with all speed." Then the beast on hearing the voice of the saint, was afraid, and fled backwards more rapidly than he came.' This first record of the monster is widely believed to be based on fact because of the proven reliability of St Adamnan's journal. (Interestingly, the monks of Fort Augustus Abbey, which is sited on the loch, and has a statue of St Columba on its east wall, recently published a book about the legend for sale to visitors. One of their number, Father Gregory, has also claimed to have sighted 'Nessie' twice.)

After the Irish monk's account, mention of the monster is very sporadic until the twentieth century: there is a reference to a 'strange sight' in Richard Frank's *Northern Memoirs* published in 1658, and Daniel Defoe reports on the 'leviathans' which disturbed soldiers building a road around the loch in 1716 in his *Tour Through the Whole Island of Great Britain*. The great Scottish collector of folklore John Francis Campbell says in his *Popular Tales of the Western Highlands* (1860) that he was told 'the loch was full of water bulls' and children were warned against playing near the edge. The first newspaper story about the monster, headed 'The Sea Serpent in the Highlands' – appeared in *The Times* of 6 March 1856 and reported that 'It has been repeatedly seen within the last fortnight by crowds of people. . . The animal is described by some as being in appearance and size like a "huge peat stack", while others affirm that a "six-oared boat" could pass between the huge fins which are occasionally visible. All, however, agree in describing its form as that of the eel; and we have heard one, whose evidence we can rely upon, state that in length he supposed it to be about 40 feet. He is currently reported to have swallowed a blanket inadvertently left on the bank of the lake by a girl herding cattle.' In subsequent years there was a steady stream of reports in various Scottish newspapers – none of which appears to have attracted more than local attention – and it was not until 1933 that the 'Loch Ness Monster' became first a national, then international, topic of interest.

It was on the afternoon of 14 April 1933 that a Mr and Mrs John Mackay were driving on the road alongside the loch from Inverness to their home in Drumnadrochit. As they approached Abriachan Mrs Mackay drew her husband's attention to a commotion on the surface of the loch, and the couple saw 'an enormous animal rolling and plunging in the water'.[69] For several minutes the dumbfounded pair watched the bizarre spectacle until the creature suddenly disappeared beneath the surface. Although they were both amazed at what they had seen, they made very little of the story when they recounted it to a friend, Mr Alex Campbell, who was the local water bailiff and a correspondent for the *Inverness Courier*. (Campbell himself later claimed to have seen the creature several times.) He naturally enough turned in a story to the editor of his paper, Dr Evan Barron, and as Nicholas Witchell has recounted in *The Loch Ness Story* (1974), 'The tale goes that when Dr. Barron saw Alex Campbell's report he said, "Well, if it is as big as Campbell says it is we can't just call it a creature; it must be a real monster." Thus the animal was christened with a title that has stuck ever since. The report of the sighting finally appeared as one of the *Courier's* leading stories in its issue of 2 May 1933, and this is traditionally credited with being the start of the long saga of the "Monster".' (According to a recent estimate, made in late 1974, there have been over 3,000 more sightings reported since that of Mr and Mrs Mackay.)

The publication of this story seems to have encouraged others who claimed to have seen the monster to come forward. Tim Dinsdale, himself now one of the most important investigators and writers on the subject – apart from

STRANGE SPECTACLE O LOCH NESS

What was it?

(FROM A CORRESPONDENT).

Loch Ness has for generations been credited with being the home of a fearsome-looking monster, but, somehow or other, the "water kelpie," as this legendary creature is called, always been regarded as a myth, if not a joke. Now, however, comes the news that the beast has been seen once more, for, on Friday of last week, a well-known business man, who lives near Inverness, and his wife (a University graduate), when motoring along the north shore of the loch, not far from Abriachan Pier, were startled to see a tremendous upheaval on the loch, which, previously, had been as calm as the proverbial mill-pond. The lady was the first to notice the disturbance, which occurred fully three-quarters of a mile from the shore, and it was her sudden cries to stop that drew her husband's attention to the water.

There, the creature disported itself, rolling and plunging for, fully a minute, its body resembling that of a whale, and the water cascading and churning like a simmering cauldron. Soon, however, it disappeared in a boiling mass of foam. Both onlookers confessed that there was something uncanny about the whole thing, for they realised that here was no ordinary denizen of the deep, because, apart from its enormous size, the beast, in taking the final plunge, sent out waves that were big enough to have been caused by a passing steamer. The watcher waited for almost half-an-hour in the hope that the monster (if such it was) would come to the surface again: but they had seen the last of it. Questioned as to the length of the beast, the lady stated that, judging by the state of water in the affected area, it seemed to be many feet long.

It will be remembered that a few years ago a party of Inverness anglers reported that, when crossing the loch in a rowing-boat, they encountered an unknown creature, whose bulk, movements, and the amount of water it displaced at once suggested that it was either a very large seal, a porpoise, or, indeed, the monster itself!

But the story, which duly appeared in print, received scant attention and less credence. In fact, most of those people who aired their views on the matter did so in a manner that bespoke feelings of the utmost scepticism.

It should be mentioned that, so far as known, neither seals or porpoises have ever been known to enter Loch Ness. Indeed, in the case of the latter, it would be utterly impossible for them to do so, and, as to the seal, it is a fact that though they have on rare occasions been seen in the River Ness, their presence in Loch Ness has never once been definitely established.

On 2 May 1933 the *Inverness Courier* printed the first news story (*above*) about the Loch Ness Monster, written by Alex Campbell (*right*)

Above right: Tim Dinsdale with a model of Nessie

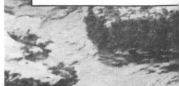

having also seen the creature – remembers what happened then:

> When this news was published it caused a great deal of interest and curiosity, and before long a flood of similar reports of sightings from people all round the Loch came in. The Monster very quickly became the centre of world-wide attention, because although television had not been introduced, radio was common, and everyone listened to "the News". Glancing back through the books and records, it is probable that some twenty or thirty sightings were published in 1933, and that these were only a small part of the total. Due to work on the new road around the Loch, sightings were often made by groups of people, and they nearly all referred to travelling waves, wakes, and humps of varying numbers, or huge backs; and occasionally a long, flexible neck would be seen breaking surface.[70]

While experts and laymen began to discuss the phenomenon – and the newspapers began to enjoy a field-day of speculation and sensation which has never really ceased – still more remarkable sightings were reported. On the afternoon of 22 July 1933 a London company director, Mr George Spicer, reported seeing 'something like a prehistoric monster' cross the Foyers Road, 200 yards ahead in front of his car. 'It seemed to have a long neck', he told newspapermen, 'which moved up and down in the manner of a scenic railway and the body was fairly big with a high back.'[71] When Mr Spicer accelerated and reached the spot on the road, the creature had disappeared into the loch – but he did remember its outline clearly enough later to produce a fascinating sketch. Another confrontation on the loch-side road which is worth mentioning occurred by moonlight on 5 January of the following year when a Mr A. Grant of Edinburgh, who was riding his motorcycle near Abriachan – the location of the first Mackay sighting – saw the creature lope across the road 'in the manner of a sea lion' and splash into the loch. He described it as '15 to 20 ft long with a small head on a long neck and bulky body and two slight humps and four flippers'.[72] When the site was inspected in daylight the following day by five Edinburgh University students a clear set of tracks was found.

Sketches were, of course, one thing: what the world really wanted was a photograph. This was duly secured on 12 November 1933. The picture was taken by a Mr Hugh Gray, an employee of the British Aluminium Company at Foyers, as he was strolling by the loch. 'An object of considerable dimensions rose out of the water not so very far from where I was,' he said in a sworn statement made later. 'I immediately got my camera ready and snapped the object which was then two to three feet above the surface of the water. I did not see any head, for what I took to be the front parts were under the water, but there was considerable movement from what seemed to be the tail, the part furthest from me. The object only appeared for a few minutes then sank out of sight.'[73] Photographic experts who examined the film were convinced that it was unretouched, and the publication of the picture in the press naturally swelled interest in the story still further. Nicholas Witchell reports: 'In a review of the events of 1933, the French press decided that the

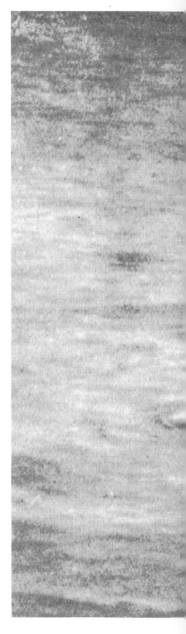

Right: The creature Mr George Spicer saw cross the Foyers Road near Loch Ness in July 1933 and (*far right*) the monster Mr A. Grant saw near Abriachan in January 1934, both illustrations from Rupert T. Gould's *The Loch Ness Monster and Others*

Below: The first photograph of the Loch Ness Monster, taken in November 1933 by Hugh Gray

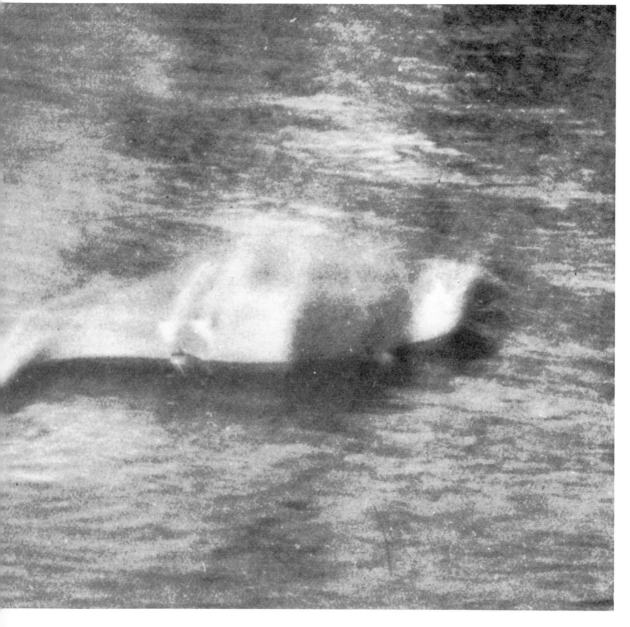

SEEN BY CAPTAIN R.A.R. MEIKLEM, R.N. (RETD) ON AUGUST 5TH, 1933, AT ABOUT 5:30 P.M. - END-VIEW OF BACK OF "MONSTER" NEAR CHERRY ISLAND, FORT AUGUSTUS. (FROM A DRAWING MADE UNDER HIS SUPERVISION)

CAPT. MEIKLEM'S SKETCH

SEEN BY MISS A. SIMPSON 40 YARDS FROM SHORE, NEAR AULTSAYE, JUNE. "MONSTER" MOVED SLOWLY: TAIL GENTLY MOVING, CAUSING FOAM. (FROM A DRAWING MADE UNDER HER SUPERVISION)

MISS SIMPSON'S SKETCH.

RAPID TURN. RAPID TURN. OBSERVED MOVEMENTS OF THE "MONSTER."

MISS GOODBODY'S SKETCH.

"MONSTER" BEING CAREFULLY OBSERVED BY MR. W.U. GOODBODY & HIS TWO DAUGHTERS FROM 11:45 A.M. TO 12:25 P.M. DECEMBER 30TH, 1933, ABOUT 2½ MILES FROM FORT AUGUSTUS. DISTANCE VARIED BETWEEN 400 & 700 YARDS. (FROM DRAWINGS MADE UNDER THEIR SUPERVISION)

PLAN OF RAPID TURN.

"MONSTER" MAKING A FINAL RAPID TURN BE BEING HIDDEN FROM VIEW IN SNOWSTORM.

FAIRLY ROUGH WATER.

AS FIRST SEEN BY MISS JANE GOODBODY; 11:45 A.M., DECEMBER 30TH, 1933, SHOWING TWO HUMPS.

AS SEEN BY THE MISSES RATTRAY & MISS HAMILTON FROM NEAR DORES, AUGUST 24TH, 1933, FOLLOWING IN THE WAKE OF THE DRIFTER "GRANT HAY". (FROM DETAIL DRAWING)

FLOATING TREE-TRUNK SEEN BY MYSELF & F OBSERVERS AT AULTSAYE ON JANUARY 4TH, 19 & THOUGHT TO BE THE "MONSTER", UNTIL USING BINOCULARS, I DISCOVERED WHAT IT REALLY W

"MONSTER'S" SIZE COMPARED WITH THE DRIFTER.

LENGTH 86 FEET.

"MONSTER" 3/4 LENGTH OF DRIFTER.

ROUGH WATER.

Two pages from a special feature which appeared in the *Illustrated London News* in January 1934 giving a pictorial round-up of the major sightings of the Loch Ness Monster to that date

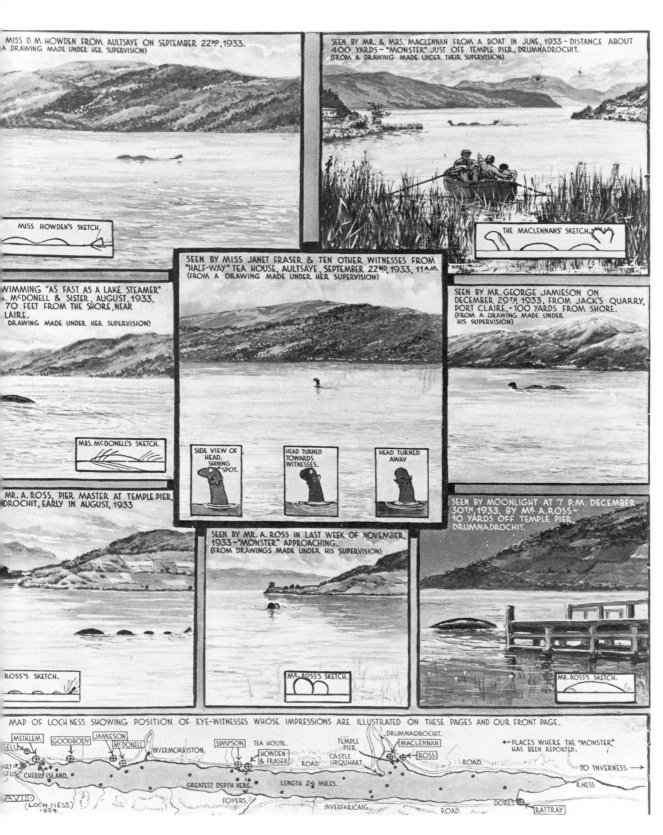

MISS D. M. HOWDEN FROM AULTSAYE ON SEPTEMBER 22ND, 1933.
(A DRAWING MADE UNDER HER SUPERVISION)

MISS HOWDEN'S SKETCH.

SEEN BY MR. & MRS. MACLENNAN FROM A BOAT IN JUNE, 1933 - DISTANCE ABOUT 400 YARDS - "MONSTER" JUST OFF TEMPLE PIER, DRUMNADROCHIT.
(FROM A DRAWING MADE UNDER THEIR SUPERVISION)

THE MACLENNANS' SKETCH.

SEEN BY MISS JANET FRASER & TEN OTHER WITNESSES FROM "HALF-WAY" TEA HOUSE, AULTSAYE, SEPTEMBER 22ND, 1933, 11 A.M.
(FROM A DRAWING MADE UNDER HER SUPERVISION)

...WIMMING "AS FAST AS A LAKE STEAMER"
... McDONELL & SISTER, AUGUST, 1933,
... 70 FEET FROM THE SHORE, NEAR ...LAIRE.
...DRAWING MADE UNDER HER SUPERVISION)

MRS. McDONELL'S SKETCH.

SIDE VIEW OF HEAD. SHINING SPOT.

HEAD TURNED TOWARDS WITNESSES.

HEAD TURNED AWAY

SEEN BY MR. GEORGE JAMIESON ON DECEMBER 29TH, 1933, FROM JACK'S QUARRY, PORT CLAIRE, - 100 YARDS FROM SHORE.
(FROM A DRAWING MADE UNDER HIS SUPERVISION)

...MR. A. ROSS, PIER MASTER AT TEMPLE PIER,
...DROCHIT, EARLY IN AUGUST, 1933

SEEN BY MR. A. ROSS IN LAST WEEK OF NOVEMBER, 1933 - "MONSTER" APPROACHING.
(FROM DRAWINGS MADE UNDER HIS SUPERVISION)

MR. ROSS'S SKETCH.

...ROSS'S SKETCH.

SEEN BY MOONLIGHT AT 7 P.M. DECEMBER 30TH, 1933, BY MR A. ROSS - 10 YARDS OFF TEMPLE PIER, DRUMNADROCHIT.

MR. ROSS'S SKETCH.

MAP OF LOCH NESS SHOWING POSITION OF EYE-WITNESSES WHOSE IMPRESSIONS ARE ILLUSTRATED ON THESE PAGES AND OUR FRONT PAGE.

MEIKLEM   GOODBODY   JAMIESON   McDONELL   INVERMORRISTON   SIMPSON   TEA HOUSE.   TEMPLE PIER   DRUMNADROCHIT.   MACLENNAN   • = PLACES WHERE THE "MONSTER" HAS BEEN REPORTED.
...ELLS   HOWDEN & FRASER   ROAD.   CASTLE URQUHART.   ROSS   ROAD.   TO INVERNESS →
...RT   CHERRY ISLAND.   GREATEST DEPTH HERE.   LENGTH 24 MILES.   R. NESS.
...TUS
...AVISS   FOYERS.   INVERFARICAIG.   ROAD.   DORES   RATTRAY
(LOCH NESS) 1934

year's only bright spot was the discovery of the Monster. The Austrian Government expressed indignation and claimed it was all an ingenious Scottish trick to keep tourists away from Austria. The British Prime Minister, Ramsay MacDonald, was reported to have been so keenly interested in the phenomenon that he planned a special trip to the Loch in the hope of catching a glimpse. At Loch Ness fishermen complained that salmon had been scarcer than normal: "Nessie" was naturally blamed.'

By the spring of 1934 the story was rapidly deteriorating into a national joke, as hoaxes and fraudulent claims of sightings fell one upon another. Those who were seriously interested in the subject – such as Rupert Gould and Constance Whyte, both of whom were to publish important works on 'Nessie' – prayed for something really substantial to halt the tide of derision. A second photograph taken on 1 April 1934 did just that. The picture had been secured by a man of enviable reputation, a London gynaecologist, Robert Kenneth Wilson, while standing with a friend on a small promontory about two miles north of Invermoriston. Subsequently it became known as the 'Surgeon's Photograph' and, according to Nicholas Witchell, 'is believed to be the only genuine picture of the head and neck of one of the animals'. In his statement, quoted by Witchell, Mr Wilson made no claims for what he had captured on film, merely that his friend had suddenly pointed to the loch and cried, 'My God, it's the Monster!' He added, 'I could not say what this object was as I was far too busy managing the camera in my amateurish way.' Those who studied the picture said it quite clearly showed the head and neck of the Loch Ness Monster.

The 'surgeon's photograph' taken by Robert Wilson in April 1934, still the best of all the pictures that have been taken

At this time a fairly wide-ranging group of 'solutions' to the monster mystery were being put forward by experts of varying qualifications. Mr E. G. Boulenger of the Zoological Society suggested that the whole thing was a result of mass-hallucination because 'for countless centuries a wealth of weird and eerie legend has centred round this great inland waterway'.[74] According to another school of thought the 'monsters' were more likely floating tree trunks, tar barrels from the road works, upturned boats or – most amazing of all – a dead elephant! Others believed natural phenomena such as aquatic birds, salmon, eels and so on lay behind the sightings, and Mr R. Elmhirst, director of the Scottish Marine Biological Association, argued that a family of otters cavorting in the water could very easily be mistaken for a monster. A strong case was also made that the creature might be a *Plesiosaurus*, or even a very large grey seal, a theory still supported by quite a number of experts today.

Although several well-organized 'expeditions', mainly armed with photographic equipment, were set up in the area in subsequent years – and continued to be mounted at regular intervals for the next twenty years – the mystery attracted far less attention after the initial excitement: mainly due, of course, to the advent of the Second World War. Sightings continued to be made and conclusions reached, and a few far from convincing photographs were taken. It was not, in fact, until 1961, when the Loch Ness Investigation Bureau was set up, that the old enthusiasms were rekindled. This organization quickly attracted members from all over the country – and even from fourteen foreign countries – and did much to foster the scientific approach to the subject which we find today. Perhaps the most important figures in the Bureau were Mr (now Sir) Peter Scott, son of the great explorer and founder of the Wildfowl Trust, and Mr Tim Dinsdale, who in the previous year had succeeded in taking 50 feet of 16 mm film of the hump of the monster weaving erratically across the loch, leaving a V-shaped wake. Although the hard work of these two men and their colleagues and supporters only succeeded in keeping the Bureau functioning until 1972, they were able to develop many of the recording and detailing techniques which are still used today by the individuals and groups who from time to time crouch on the banks of the loch with the most sophisticated photographic and recording equipment at the ready, or else cruise the waters with sonar devices and stroboscopic cameras to pick up any movements below.

It has been just such dedicated work that has resulted in the very latest development in this ages-old mystery – the publication of a series of coloured photographs taken underwater by an American team led by Dr Robert Rines of the Academy of Applied Sciences in Boston and heralded in some quarters as 'finally proving beyond doubt that "Nessie" exists'.[75] Sir Peter Scott has greeted the pictures, each depicting different parts of a huge creature, as genuine, and has even produced a remarkable painting of what he believes *two* of the creatures look like: and indeed it is now being suggested by some authorities – including no less a person than Jacques Cousteau, the world-famous

Sir Peter Scott's painting
of two Loch Ness Monsters,
completed in 1975

marine biologist – that there is almost certainly a whole family of such monsters in the depths of the loch. Nevertheless, some experts still remain unconvinced by the photographs, and doubtless until an actual monster is caught – or at least the carcass of one examined – the mystery will continue to fascinate everyone as it has for centuries.

The Loch Ness Monster is far from being unique, as I mentioned at the start of this chapter, and indeed, as Sir Peter Scott confirms in an article he wrote in the *Sunday Times* in 1960, 'There is great fascination in the stories of "beasties" not only in Loch Ness, but also in Lochs Morar, Shiel, Quoich, and in Ireland (not forgetting lakes in Iceland, Manitoba and British Columbia), all of which may claim connection, through relatives in the sea lochs and fjords, with the equally debatable sea-serpent.' I should now like to consider a few of the other more important creatures of this kind within the scope of this book.

America has a long history of water monsters, both on inland lakes and off her coasts, and there are several stories of these creatures in the traditions of such great Indian tribes as the Crees, Algonquins, Onandagas and Ojibways.

One of the earliest reports in English deals with a thirty-five-foot-long monster 'with bright eyes'[76] seen on Lake Erie in July 1817. Not long after this, records indicate, several similar tales began to be heard in the state of Wisconsin: an obnoxiously smelly creature was said to live in Rock Lake, and an 'undulating form like a huge snake or fish with a row of protuberances like a saw tooth along its back'[77] frightened residents of Red Cedar Lake, while the 'sea serpent' in Lake Monona, which was at first thought to be a hoax, has continued to be reported to the present day. In 1886 a monster reared its head out of the Great Sandy Lake in Minnesota, and was promptly fired upon by a hunter named Christopher Egstein who happened to be passing at that moment. His action, plus a number of other similar stories of monsters in lakes in the western mountain states, including the legendary creature in Bear Lake, Utah, which had legs and could crawl on land, are believed to have been the inspiration for a dramatic story, *The Monster of Lake La Metrie* by Wardon Allan Curtis, which enjoyed some notoriety when it was published in 1899.

Interesting though these stories are, they remain essentially disappointing, as Peter Costello remarks in his authoritative work *In Search of Lake Monsters* (1974): 'However convincing this long tradition of lake monsters in the United States may be, stretching as it does all the way across the continent for a century and a half, the reports lack any physical evidence to support them. There is nothing we can consider apart from the reports; no photographs, no drawings, no alleged remains.' For visual evidence from the American continent, in fact, we need to refer to the coastal areas and in particular New England – where apparently as early as 1638 there was considerable discussion in Boston concerning the birth of a 'monster', and also the unexpected arrival of a sea serpent off Cape Ann.

Far and away the most important sighting, however, occurred in August 1817, when a sea serpent was seen by numerous people in the New England fishing-port of Gloucester. The story is notable both because a drawing of the creature was produced and because an official enquiry was conducted by a local three-man committee. According to one of the most exact eye-witnesses, a local mariner named Amos Story, he first saw the sight with a spyglass at about midday on 10 August near Ten Pound Island. 'His head appeared shaped much like the head of the sea turtle, and he carried his head from ten to twelve inches above the surface of the water,' the old man said. 'His head at that distance appeared larger than the head of any dog that I ever saw. From the back part of his head to the next part of him that was visible, I should judge to be three or four feet. He moved very rapidly through the water, I should say a mile in two, or at most, in three minutes.' Unlike most of his kind, the creature stayed in Amos's view for an hour and half, and the good man was to see him again: 'I likewise saw what I believe to be the same animal this day, viz. the twenty third of August. This was in the morning, about seven o'clock. He then lay perfectly still, extended on the water, and I should judge that I saw fifty feet of him at least.' Eleven other witnesses were to give their sworn

Left: An illustration of the
monster of Lake La Metrie
from *Pearson's Magazine,*
September 1899

statements to the investigators, and it emerged that the creature had first appeared in the district on 6 August. All agreed that it was dark brown in colour, about seventy feet long, and had 'joints from his head to his tail'. It had frequented the harbour for about a fortnight, and, noted the committee, had been 'repeatedly observed by many persons – sometimes at exceedingly close range'. A ship's carpenter named Matthew Gaffney, who was out in a rowing boat at the time of one of these appearances, believed the creature was about to attack him and shot at it without apparent success. As a result of this incident a number of local fishermen made a net with which to try and catch the serpent, and several boatloads of seamen spent many hours 'well manned and armed' searching the harbour. The enquirers were of the opinion that Amos Story was probably the last man to see the creature in Gloucester, and that shortly after 23 August it left the vicinity 'being seen five days later eastward of Cape Ann, heading away from Gloucester, and passing rapidly north-eastward along the coast'.[78] Thereafter the 'New England Sea Serpent' passed into legend, although I have learned that sightings of a similar nature were recorded along this same stretch of coast right up to the turn of the century.

In a recent article in the publication *Man, Myth and Magic* (1971) the folklore expert Eric Maple reports that things have not changed much in the twentieth century: 'Fantastic monsters from the primeval deep have continued to terrorise the American coastal region as well as the inland waters. In the 1930's a huge "grey thing" emerged from the 60-feet-deep river at Newport, Arkansas, bringing hordes of sightseers into the area. Yet another fantastic marine monster 18 feet long was captured at Sandusky, Ohio in 1931, and was put on public exhibition by two enterprising salesmen. Even more outstanding was the gigantic "toad-headed" horror which protruded its head above the sea just enough to be photographed off San Diego Bay.'

Canada has a similarly rich tradition of water creatures, the serpent known as the Ogopogo, which makes its home in Lake Okanagan on the Pacific slopes of the Rockies in British Columbia, being perhaps the most remarkable. In this sixty-nine-mile-long stretch of water there is a small, barren island, and it is here that the Ogopogo is said to live. The serpent has apparently been a subject of much interest since the days when only the Indians lived in the vicinity and called it Naitaka – 'the monster spirit of the lake'. They regarded the creature with superstitious awe and from time to time left sacrifices of small animals to appease its wrath. Indeed there are numerous stories of the Ogopogo feeding on unwilling victims, including a team of horses that a settler was swimming across the lake in 1854. According to eye-witnesses who had seen the creature it was 'at least 20 feet long, and had a heavy snake-like body, a horse's head and was well-bearded.'[79] The Ogopogo appears to have been given its later name by a journalist in 1872 when the first important modern sightings were reported, and by 1924 it was even the star of a music hall song which ran:

His mother was an earwig,
His father was a whale.

Above: Three illustrations from *The Great Sea Serpent* by A. C. Dudemans *Top:* The serpent witnessed by the crew of the steamer *Katie* near the Hebrides in May 1882. *Centre:* The Galveston sea serpent reported by Mr Walthew, a Liverpool ship owner, in May 1872. *Bottom:* The famous Boston serpent

A little bit of head
And hardly any tail,
And Ogopogo was his name.

It was in the late 1940s that stories of the creature began to proliferate – alleged tracks even being found on the shore – and in 1950 Mr and Mrs Bruce Miller had a remarkable view of it, as Mr Miller described later. 'It was a lithe, sinewy monster, 75 feet in length with a coiled back and dignified demeanour. Periodically his progress would be halted as he lay quietly on the water, head well raised, and surveyed the lake with calm dignity.'[80] Other witnesses, including no less a person than the German Vice-Consul in Vancouver, Hans Gerade, have continued to report seeing the creature to this day, and it undoubtedly deserves monster-hunter Peter Costello's endorsement: 'Even those of us who have not been lucky enough to see Ogopogo can be persuaded of its existence by the evidence of witnesses. Lake Okanagan . . . is the Canadian Loch Ness.'[81]

Other lake monsters have also been reported in the Great Lakes, and there is a creature 'with a saw-tooth fin down the centre'[82] in Mocking Lake, Quebec, which several eye-witnesses have tried unsuccessfully to shoot. Similarly there are persistent tales of a creature 'with a single horn protruding from the back of its head like a periscope'[83] which lives in the group of interconnected lakes around Winnipeg and was the object of a zoological expedition in 1960. Canada's best known sea serpent is *Cadborosaurus* – 'Caddy' for short – which was first brought to public attention in the 1930s, although it was a traditional figure in the legends of the Chinook Indians. There is an impressive list of over a hundred people who claim to have seen this strange beast in the vicinity of Cadbury Bay (hence its name) in the Chatham Islands of British Columbia – perhaps the most important evidence being that of Mr F. W. Kemp, an archivist, whose sketch of what he saw in August 1932 is reproduced here. Mr Kemp was holidaying with his wife and son when they saw 'a mysterious something with its head out of the water' coming towards them. The serpent made a very loud noise and then 'fold after fold of its body came to the surface'. Mr Kemp went on, 'The Thing's presence seemed to change the whole landscape, which makes it difficult to describe my experiences. It did not seem to belong to the present scheme of things, but rather to the Long Ago when the world was young.' He estimated the creature to be at least eighty feet long, with a body more than five feet thick, and it was of a bluish-green colour 'which shone in the sunshine like aluminium'.[84] In some subsequent reports it was said that there was a second creature in the vicinity, in all probability 'Caddy's' mate!

Australia can also claim several strange creatures, including the mysterious Bunyip which inhabits a number of rivers and lakes and whose name is an Aborigine word meaning 'water devil'. Descriptions of the Bunyip vary considerably: Mr E. S. Hall in the *Sydney Gazette* of 3 March 1823 said that it 'made a noise like a porpoise and had a bulldog's head', while another report

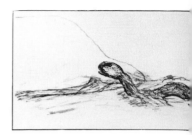

Above: Sketch by Mr F. W. Kemp of the monster 'Caddy' he saw near the Chatham Islands, Canada (*right*)

Below: Drawing of the sea serpent sighted off South Africa in 1896, from Dudemans' *The Great Sea Serpent*

of 1847 said it has a human face and its feet were turned backwards! Reports of sightings have been made from numerous places including Swan River, Lake Bathurst, Lake George, Lake Parker, the Midgion Lagoon near Narrandera, River Mongolo, and the Tuckerbill Swamp near Leeton where it was alleged there lived a Bunyip with two heads which could reverse direction without turning round! According to reports one of these creatures was actually caught in the Port Fairy District of Victoria in 1848, with a long neck, shaggy mane and a head like a kangaroo – but, like a number of alleged eye-witnesses' drawings of the Bunyip, all traces of this 'catch' have long since disappeared. There have been a number of scientific expeditions to try and get at the truth of the Bunyip, and while it has been suggested by the zoologist Gilbert Whitely that it may be 'an extinct marsupial otter-like animal',[85] this remains to be proved, and the reports which still come in only serve to heighten the mystery: a group of picnickers near Wagga Wagga in January 1960, for example, said the creature swam by using its long ears as paddles! The continent's sea creature is the Moha Moha, which appears off Queensland and was first reported in the nineteenth century. It was described as having a 'huge, dome-shaped body, long neck with flat head, and a tail of about 12 feet' by a reader of the magazine *Land and Water* in 1891. According to Miss S. Lovell, the major investigator into the Moha Moha legend, the first theories were that the creature was a giant turtle, but eye-witness reports credited it with behaviour not in keeping with this species – including attacks on human beings – and the consensus of opinion was that it was half-fish and half-turtle. Miss Lovell herself saw the creature for half an hour, and wrote later: 'In moving about, head and tail were seen alternately above water, but not even the shadow of its great body, and, from the length of that, a spectator could not guess that the head and tail belonged to the same creature, particularly as the colouring is so different.'[86]

These, then, are just some of the more important aquatic creatures, and indeed the number of reports of their existence from around the world are only rivalled by the variety of theories as to their real nature: relics from a bygone age, cases of mistaken identity, mass hallucination, inanimate objects and so on. It has long been maintained that proof of their existence will only emerge when the body of one is found, or when at least some samples of its skin can be obtained and tested.

Though none of our more famous 'beasties' have yet been so obliging, there are two recent instances of bodies turning up which I should just like to mention briefly, particularly as we have photographic evidence to back up the accounts. The first occurred at Santa Cruz in California in May 1925 when a huge carcass was washed up on the beach. Among the many eye-witnesses who saw the body was a zoologist, Dr David Jordan, who said it was 'thirty seven feet long with a long, thin neck and a huge, distended head'. According to Dr Jordan's report published shortly afterwards the creature had a 'mouth like the bill of a duck, the eyes were just pimples, and on the end of its big body was a curly tail'.[87] Dr Jordan was unable to offer an explanation as to

Today the Daily Mirror publishes the controversial pictures from Loch Ness

Nessie, is this REALLY you?

By ARTHUR SMITH, Science Correspondent

SO this is what all that fuss was about ... the much-heralded proof that Nessie lives.

These are the pictures taken by a team of American scientists last summer, using an electronic flash 45ft. below the surface of Loch Ness.

The pictures weren't even this clear at first. They have been sharpened by a system known as computer-enhancement.

That full-body study on the left may look to you like a bursting haggis thrown over the side of a loch steamer.

But it's good enough to convince Sir Peter Scott, the painter and wildfowl expert, and Dr. Robert Rines, the Boston attorney who led the American team.

In Britain's leading scientific journal Nature, where the monster picture was first published yesterday, they even put forward a name for Nessie.

They called it Nessiteras Rhombopteryx — which means the Ness Monster with a diamond-shaped fin — and explained that if it

THE SYSTEM: How computer enhancement works. The picture, left, of Mars satellite Phobus was taken by a Mariner spacecraft in 1971. It was fed into a computer which created the new, clearer close-up, right. The same process was used on the Nessie pictures.

wasn't named it couldn't become a protected species under British law.

Sir Peter and the doctor calculate that their monster is anything up to 65ft. long, living on fish and plant debris. And they reckon Nessies have been breeding in the loch ever since it ceased to be an arm of the sea 12,000 years ago.

The pair defended their evidence before a slightly sceptical Press conference in London last night. Dr. Rines calling his monster "the tenth wonder of the world."

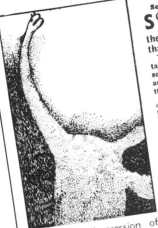

An artist's impression of how the monster, left, looks.

The hunt for the Loch Ness Monster continues! Nessie hits the headlines in December 1975 following the release of new photographs taken by the American, Dr Robert Rines

Opposite above: Frank Searle, who has spent over 20,000 hours watching the loch and claims twenty-four sightings

Opposite below: The latest in a long line of expeditions – a Japanese team takes to the water, 1976

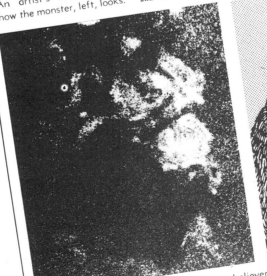

The splodge that believers call the head, with horns which may be schnorkel tubes—clearly shown in the artist's version—for breath without causing a ripple on the loch.

Graphics by TERRY D

HEAD

154

Below: The huge rotten carcass that was found on Prah Sands in Cornwall in June 1928

Above: A remarkable photograph of the head of a sea monster which was washed up on the beach at Santa Cruz in California in May 1925

what the creature might be, but could not accept the only theory offered, that it was possibly the decomposed carcass of a rare Baird's beaked whale. On 7 June 1928 a still more rotten corpse was found on Prah Sands in Cornwall with a body measuring thirty feet in length but minus its head. The carcass had four small flippers which appeared to be for swimming, and a tail which tapered to a point. Its skin was dirty white in colour, coarse to the touch and covered with hair or bristles. Again, the experts who viewed the body could reach no definite conclusions, and the lame suggestion that it might be the remains of a basking shark was quickly dismissed. So, as in the Santa Cruz case, the question still remained: was this the body of some unknown monster of the deeps? How long we may have to wait for the answers is anyone's guess.

Right: A Japanese drawing of the Loch Ness Monster

Filming the Loch Ness Monster
An extract from *The Story of the Loch Ness Monster*
by Tim Dinsdale, London 1973

EARLY ON the Saturday morning of April 23rd, 1960, returning from a dawn-watch further down the loch, I spotted something large far out on the water.

I was in my car, with the camera mounted on a tripod beside me in place of the front seat which I had removed. I was overlooking Foyers Bay at a point about 300 ft. up the mountainside. It was just before nine o'clock, and the water was calm, and the air clear as crystal.

The sun shone on the object, and I could see it was a reddish-brown colour.

Stopping the car at the roadside I lifted my binoculars and examined it carefully. Enlarged seven times, I could see it much better. It was not a boat, and it was quite motionless.

Suddenly it came to life, and surged away across the water, with ripples breaking away from the farther end. I could see now that it was the back of a great animal – a strange humped back, and on the left side of it there was a curious dark blotch. There was no fin on the back – as with a whale, or a porpoise – of that I was certain.

Turning to my camera, I shot about forty feet of film of the Monster as it zig-zagged its way across the loch, gradually submerging.

When fully submerged it turned abruptly left underwater, and swam close to the far shore for perhaps a quarter of a mile, throwing up the great V-wash I had read about, and which the man had described to me three days previously.

With only fifteen feet of film remaining, I stopped the camera, and raced with it in the car down the mountainside, out over a field towards the shore hoping to get a much closer view of the Monster; but when I arrived at the water's edge there was nothing to be seen for miles in each direction – just the glassy surface. The Monster had dived back into the depths!

Disappointed, I returned to eat my breakfast, then arranged for the hotel owner to take out a rowing-boat with a small outboard engine, so that I could film it for comparison. Obviously, if a boat of the kind used on Loch Ness appeared in the same film, after the Monster, it would at least prove the object wasn't a boat. This comparison was vitally important.

Later, back in England, I had the film developed carefully by Kodak, and in the weeks that followed it was shown privately to a number of people; but it was not until it was seen on television – on Richard Dimbleby's famous *Panorama* programme of June 13th, 1960 – that the Loch Ness Monster again became a matter of popular interest and serious discussion.

Nearly ten million people had watched the interview, and seen the film for themselves.

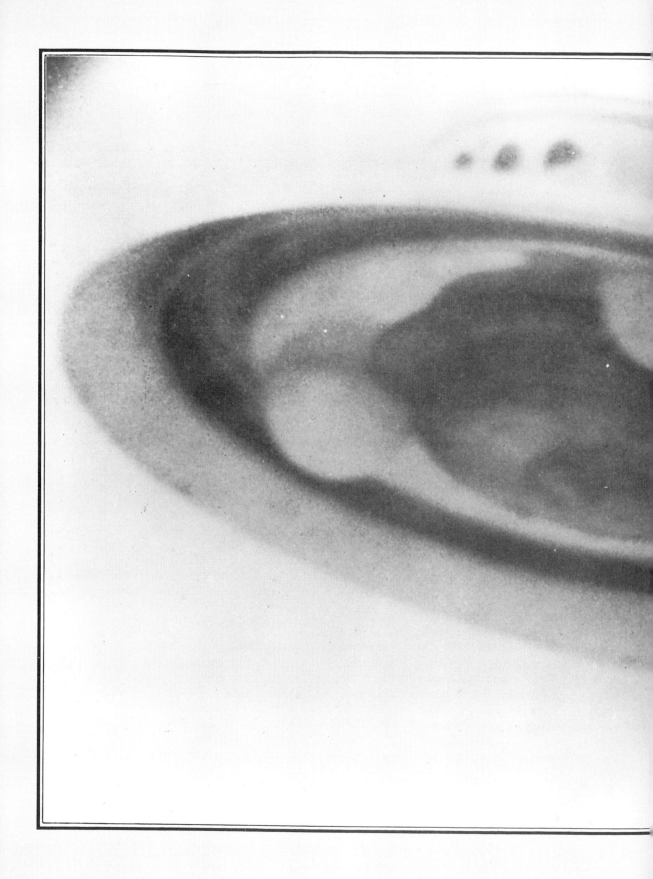

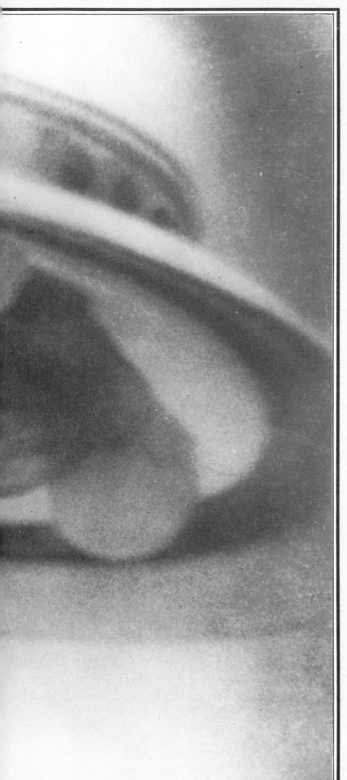

X
VISITORS FROM OUTER SPACE

George Adamski's famous photograph of a
Flying Saucer taken in California in December
1952

Right: Aerial phenomenon
observed over Basel in 1566

Below right: The flying
machine seen by P. Kettle
over Peterborough in 1909

Flying saucers – or Unidentified
Flying Objects (UFOs), as they are officially called – are for many people the
latest phenomenon to join the ranks of the inexplicable. Yet, for others, they
are as steeped in legend as any topic we have covered in this book – strange,
silent presences that have been known to man, though misunderstood by
him, from the very earliest times. According to this school of thought those
who ride in the Flying Saucers are superior beings who have played an important part in the build-up of civilizations, the construction of mighty edifices
around the world, and the performance of the 'miracles' associated with the
great religions. Needless to say this whole topic is one of enormous controversy – even the actuality of UFOs is widely disputed – and as it is currently
attracting more attention than any other subject we have dealt with in this
book, it makes a most suitable finale to our study.

Although I propose to refer to all these 'objects seen in the sky' as Flying
Saucers, it needs to be pointed out that this name is of very recent origin – as
recent as 24 June 1947, in fact, when an American pilot, Kenneth Arnold,
described something he had seen as 'a formation of very bright objects . . . that
flew like a saucer would if you skipped it across the water'[88] and in so doing
added an evocative new term to our language. However, if we turn to historical records, and accept the modern interpretation put on accounts therein,
we can find descriptions of these self-same aerial craft going back through
many centuries. First, though, we shall concern ourselves simply with authen-
ticated sightings, returning later to the advocates of the 'super beings' theory
and their explanations of legendary sightings.

According to W. R. Drake in his *Spacemen in the Middle Ages* (1964), 'The
belief in Beings from the Skies who surveyed our Earth persisted in human
consciousness throughout the Middle Ages.' He cites over three hundred
documented sightings prior to the twentieth century, with one of the earliest
from an English-speaking nation being that on the night of 1 January 1254
when, according to Matthew of Paris in his *Historia Anglorum*, a group of
monks at St Albans saw in the sky 'a kind of large ship, elegantly shaped, and
well equipped and of marvellous colour'. A perhaps more specific reference
is given for the year 1290, when the abbot and monks at Byland Abbey in
Yorkshire saw a 'large round silver disc fly slowly over them'.[89] During this
same period, and on through the next three hundred years, Europe enjoyed a
great many similar sightings, perhaps the most notable being the 'aerial

'phenomenon' seen over Basel on 7 August 1566.

The great astronomer Sir Edmund Halley reported seeing a bright object in the sky over London for more than two hours in March 1716; and two years later Sir Hans Sloane, who became President of the Royal Society, was eye-witness to 'a great light which at first I thought was only a rocket but it moved more slowly than a falling star in a direct line'.[90] A hundred years later, the first reports of aerial sights were being made in America: in 1833, for instance, a 'large, luminous craft' was seen for more than an hour over the Niagara Falls, according to Charles Fort in *The Books of Charles Fort* (1941). Fort also reports that in April 1897 more than 10,000 people saw an airship over Kansas City, Missouri. 'Object appeared very swiftly,' he writes, 'then appeared to stop and hover over the city for ten minutes at a time, then after flashing green-blue and white lights, shot upwards into space.' A similar craft is also reported to have been seen later that month over Iowa, Michigan, Nebraska, Wisconsin and Illinois, where, according to the *Chicago Record*, it actually landed in fields near Carlinville, 'but took off immediately some people approached close to it'. A personal encounter with what may have been the same object was described in a sworn statement made by a Mr Alexander Hamilton of Le Roy, Kansas, who said that on the night of 21 April 1897 he was awakened by a strange craft descending outside his farm. 'It consisted of a great cigar-shaped portion, possibly three hundred feet long, with a carriage underneath,' said Mr Hamilton, a member of the House of Representatives. 'The carriage was made of glass or some other transparent substance alternating with a narrow strip of material. It was brilliantly lighted within and everything was plainly visible – it was occupied by six of the strangest beings I ever saw. They were jabbering together, but I could not understand a word they said.' When Mr Hamilton and two of his men came out into the open, the strange beings immediately 'turned on some unknown power' and the craft soared away.[91] Despite much derision, Mr Hamilton never retracted a word of his statement.

Progressing into the twentieth century we find a whole series of sightings reported in Great Britain in May 1909, and these, says Jacques Vallée in his *Anatomy of a Phenomenon* (1965), 'were perhaps the first "wave" reported as such'. Mr Vallée goes on: '*The Weekly Dispatch* of May 23 1909, published a list of twenty-two towns "visited" by flying objects between May 16 and May 23, and nineteen towns visited before that period.' The author tells us that the spring of 1909 also provided the first twentieth-century report of a landing and a description of the spacemen who piloted the craft. 'The encounter is said to have taken place on May 18 at 11 p.m. at Caerphilly, Wales,' he writes. 'The witness, a Mr Lethbridge, said he had been walking along a road when he saw a large cylindrical object, alongside of which were two men wearing fur coats, who spoke in an excited voice when they saw the witness. Immediately afterwards they took off and the object disappeared.' In his book *The Flying Saucer Story* (1966) Brinsley Le Poer Trench says that there was also a spate of reports of cigar-shaped objects seen over New Zealand in 1909:

'During a six-week period from the last week in July to the first week in September, hundreds of eye-witnesses reported airships in the skies over New Zealand. The objects were seen by residents in both North Island and South Island. They were sighted both by day and by night.' Canada similarly received a string of visitations by five or six groups of flying objects in February 1913. According to Professor Chant in the spring 1913 issue of the *Journal of the Royal Astronomical Association of Canada* they could be compared to an aerial fleet manoeuvering. 'On February 10', he added, 'the dark objects were seen in Toronto in the afternoon, flying in three groups from west to east, and later returning in disorder. They were too distant for the observers to determine their nature, but they were not clouds or birds or smoke.'

In the years between the two World Wars, flying objects continued to be seen in locations all over the world from the heart of Europe to the depths of Russia, and from the wastes of Greenland to the lush jungles of South America. One notable contact occurred in 1931, when a Mr Francis Chichester, later to win world fame for his lone voyages, was flying a tiny Moth aeroplane across the Tasmanian Sea from New South Wales, Australia, and saw from his open cockpit 'a dull grey-white airship approaching'. Writing later in his book *The Lonely Sea and the Sky* (1964) he recalled, 'It was pearl-shaped, flashing brightly, periodically vanishing, re-appearing, accelerating and finally disappearing.'

During the Second World War there were a great variety of reported sightings which really require a book on their own – particularly because of the circumstances under which they were made, the armaments then being employed, and the emotional and physical stresses affecting the combatants. Certainly there are many fascinating accounts by Allied airmen of mysterious, silent escorts they had during bombing raids over Germany. They even coined a name for them, 'Foo Fighters', and some thought they were of German origin – just as, conversely, the Germans, who had similar encounters, supposed that the objects were British or American! In any event, one can do no better, I think, than recommend the reader interested in this period to consult the veritable library of books on UFOs which now exists, and, having done so, move on to the Kenneth Arnold sighting in 1947 which began the modern phase of what has been termed 'UFOlogy'.

Arnold, who was a fire appliance salesman by profession, was also a skilled pilot who from time to time took part in rescue work – and it was on just such a mission that he was engaged during the afternoon of 24 June 1947. He had taken off from Chehalis Airport, Washington, to look for a C-46 Marine Transport plane that had crashed somewhere in the Cascade Mountains. It was a bright, clear day, and as he began to circle over an area where the lost plane might have been a flash of light caught his eye. He relates what happened next in the privately published book he wrote with Ray Palmer, *The Coming of the Saucers* (1952), 'I observed far to my left and to the North a formation of nine very bright objects coming from the vicinity of Mount Baker, flying very close to the mountain tops and travelling with tremendous speed. I

Silver Balls Floating in Air Nazis' Newest War Device 1944

(The Associated Press)

Paris, Dec. 13.—As the Allied armies ground out new gains on the western front today, the Germans were disclosed to have thrown a new "device" into the war—mysterious silvery balls which float in the air.

Pilots report seeing these objects, both individually and in clusters, during forays over the Reich.

(The purpose of the floaters was not immediately evident. It is possible that they represent a new anti-aircraft defense instrument or weapon.)

(This dispatch was heavily censored at supreme headquarters.)

Left: A report about 'Foo Fighters' which appeared in the *New Orleans Item* of December 1944

Below: An advertisement for the book that began the modern interest in Flying Saucers, and (*below left*) front cover of an issue of Ray Palmer's magazine

SPECIAL **FLYING SAUCER** ISSUE!..., See Page 4

AMAZING STORIES

IS THE GOVERNMENT HIDING SAUCER FACTS?
Raymond Palmer Says, Yes!

"OUTER SPACE SAUCERS—A MYTH!"
By Oliver P. Ferrell

"THE ALIENS ARE AMONG US!"
By Gray Barker

Richard Shaver
Rev. Neal Harvey
Many Others

The COMING *of the* SAUCERS!

At last! The authentic story of the mysterious sky objects that have shaken the complacency of the world. On-the-spot answers to the top question of the century.

By the two men who know most about them!

KENNETH ARNOLD & RAY PALMER'S DOCUMENTARY REPORT TO THE WORLD

An amazing array of factual evidence, gathered under incredible difficulties and actual risk of life, shorn of the official "smog" that has hidden the truth from the very outset. An incredible array of evidence — the result of over four years of investigation.

The Only Book That Tells The
WHOLE TRUTH
AND NOTHING BUT THE TRUTH!

No trickery, no practical jokes, no "top secret", no "classification"! Here are the simple, unadorned, dramatic facts. A documentary record of unimpeachable honesty.

PRIVATELY PRINTED—NO CENSORSHIP!
LIMITED EDITION

ORDER YOUR COPY TODAY

PRICE $4.00

ORDER NOW FROM
RAY PALMER
AMHERST, WISCONSIN
Only Prepaid Orders Accepted

could see no tails on them and they flew like no aircraft I had ever seen before.'
As he watched in amazement, Arnold tried to judge their speed by timing how
quickly they passed from one mountain range to another. He knew the
distances well enough from past experience – and was astonished to estimate
they must be travelling at well over 1,300 mph! When the erratic course of
the objects finally took them out of his vision, he turned slowly back towards
base, all thoughts of the missing plane gone from his mind.

The story of Arnold's sighting soon became national and international news,
and in succeeding weeks a number of eye-witnesses on the ground and several
airline pilots in the skies claimed to have seen craft similar to those spotted
over the Cascade Mountains. At first the American authorities attempted to
ignore the whole matter, but when six objects were reported from an official
military source, these same authorities reacted with amazing speed, as Charles
Bowen, editor of the influential magazine *Flying Saucer Review* has commented: 'Despite widely spread rumours of the sightings, a communique was
issued on July 4 1947 in which it was stated that the experiences must have
been hallucinatory. And so the seal was set on the official attitude to UFO
reports for years to come, an example that in time was publicly followed by
authorities right round the world when their turn came to be faced with
reports of this kind.' As Mr Bowen points out, barely had this statement been
issued than there were fresh sightings reported from Washington, Idaho,
Oregon, and even Canada, where the witnesses were men of the highest
integrity. 'That all these witnesses suffered from the same hallucination', he
says, 'would seem to be beyond the bounds of medical probability.'[92]

As the months passed, the reports continued to pour in and officialdom
tried other explanations for the UFOs. (This term, which was the designation
given to the craft by the United States Air Force, was at least an indication that
somebody somewhere thought there must be something in the stories.) Time
and time again the 'explanation' was put forward that a military aircraft had
been sighted – only to be disproved when the Air Force admitted that none
of their planes had been in the area in question. Then escaped weather balloons
were suggested – but again no record to substantiate any such loss could be
found – as were meteors, low-hanging clouds, ball lightning, migrating birds,
large hailstones, and even the planet Venus! By the following year, however,
even the authorities admitted that there was a small percentage of sightings
for which no explanation could be offered, and consequently the U.S. Government set up Project Sign (later retitled Project Blue Book) to collate and examine information. For years this project, which was the responsibility of the
Air Force, debunked one sighting after another, despite overwhelming evidence
to the contrary. Then, in 1969, the organization tried to wrap up the whole
issue with the publication of the Condon Report. This, as Jeremy Pascall
commented in an article, 'Who Believes in UFOs?', 'was the result of the
work of a committee set up under Dr Edward V. Condon to scientifically
assess the evidence regarding UFOs. Given £250,000 and, it later transpired,
a secret directive on the line to take, Condon came up with what was intended

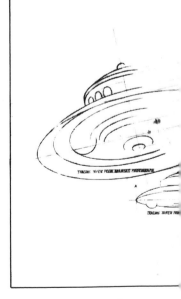

Above: Comparative drawings
based on Adamski's photograph
and on a photograph taken
by schoolboy Stephen
Darbyshire

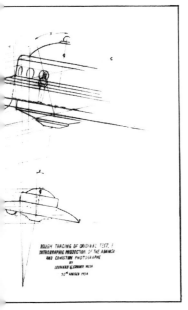

Top: Another view of the
Flying Saucer photographed
by George Adamski in
1952

to be the final refutation of UFOs.'[93] Summing up the essence of the 965 pages
of the report Dr Condon wrote, 'Our general conclusion is that nothing has
come from the study of UFOs in the past 21 years that has added to scientific
knowledge. Careful consideration of the record as it is available to us leads us
to conclude that further extensive study of UFOs probably cannot be justified
in the expectation that science will be advanced thereby.'[94] But if the doctor
expected his to be the last word, the continuing growth of interest in UFOs
has surely proved him quite mistaken.

Aside from the eye-witness accounts, those interested in the phenomenon
both in America and abroad were starting to assemble quite an impressive
collection of photographs of UFOs. Some of the pictures of saucer-shaped
craft proved to be tricks of the light, double exposures or deliberate fraud,
but there were others that passed virtually all the tests that could be applied.
Perhaps the most remarkable of all the pictures, though there still remain some
doubts about them, were the series of close-ups of a saucer taken at Mount
Palomar, California, in December 1952. The photographer was an amateur
astronomer named George Adamski who took the picture through a six-inch
Tinsley reflecting telescope when the saucer was hovering about 3,000 feet
above. Mr Adamski claimed to have seen similar objects on several other
occasions and even to have established contact with the 'aliens' who rode in
them. He later recounted these experiences in a remarkable book, now looked
upon as something of a classic in UFOlogy, *Flying Saucers Have Landed* (1953).
In England a thirteen-year-old schoolboy, Stephen Darbyshire, also took a
remarkable picture of a saucer which he came across while walking on the
slopes of Coniston in the Lake District in February 1954. Not long afterwards
these pictures were seemingly surpassed by a photograph taken by a Mr
Cedric Allingham, which, he claimed, showed a Martian about to enter a
Flying Saucer. Mr Allingham, an enthusiastic birdwatcher, had been pursuing
his hobby on a lonely stretch of the northern Scottish coast near Lossiemouth
when the craft landed and the spaceman got out for a few moments. Sceptics
were unable to take the picture very seriously because, they said, the 'spaceman' appeared to be wearing trousers held up by a rather obvious pair of
braces! Mr Allingham also wrote a book about his experiences called *Flying
Saucers from Mars* (1955).

According to Charles Bowen, UFO sightings have followed a fairly precise
pattern during their history. 'There is a distinct "wave" phenomenon about
the incidence of UFO's with well-defined peaks of activity,' he says. 'Modern
interest started in 1947, and there were waves in 1948 and 1952, in 1957 and
1958, in 1962–63, in 1964, 1967 and so on. Researchers into the history of the
subject have also unearthed newspaper reports of big waves in 1946 – the
"ghost rockets" over Sweden when people thought the objects were captured
German rocket weapons being tested by the Russians – in 1943–44 – the spate
known as "Foo Fighters" – in 1934, 1913, 1909, 1896–7 (mystery "airships"
over California and the Middle West) and earlier. The most concentrated, and
sensational, of all waves to date was that of 1954.'[95]

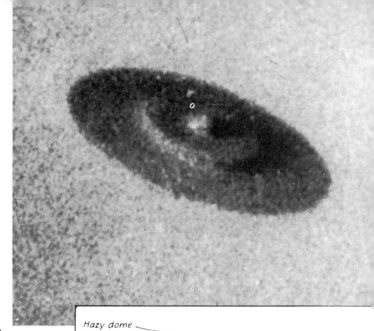

Hazy dome

Clean cut sharp edge

Halo appeare on take-o

MAN IN A FLYING SAUCER

We spoke to him, women claim

OSLO, Tuesday.

TWO Norwegian sisters claim to have spoken to a man who landed by flying saucer, said a police chief in Mosjoen, Central Norway, today.

This, according to the newspaper *Helgeland*, is their story:

The sisters, aged 24 and 32, were out in the hills picking berries. A dark, long-haired man wearing a kind of khaki overall without buttons appeared. He motioned them to a hollow.

He seemed friendly enough, so they went. There on the ground was the flying saucer, about 16ft. in diameter. The man tried vainly with words, gestures, and drawings to explain himself.

Three languages

The women tried French, German, and English without success. Then the stranger climbed into the saucer. It started up with a slight humming sound like a bumble bee, rose at great speed straight into the air—and vanished.

Police are to visit the spot tomorrow to see if they can find any trace of the saucer.—Reuter.

D.M. Paris cable: Three people have reported seeing a "flying saucer" attached to a huge cigar-shaped object over the Seine at Evreux, north-west of Paris. It was watched for 45 minutes.

FLYING SAUCER

From a laundry in Rochdale

SILENTLY . . . ominously . . . The Thing hovered over a Lancashire village. It glowed a ghostly white.

Villagers at Wardle, near Rochdale, cried: "It's a flying saucer!"

Was it? The answer came in the Commons yesterday when Mr. J. A. Leavey (C. Heywood and Royton) asked whether the Air Minister knew about The Thing.

Amid laughter, Mr. Charles Orr-Ewing, Parliamentary Under-Secretary, replied: "This object, which was described in the Press as a flying saucer, did not emanate from outer space, but from a laundry in Rochdale."

Just 2 Balloons

"It consisted of two small hydrogen-filled balloons illuminated by a flashlight bulb and devised by a laundry mechanic."

Last night the man who made The Thing, Neil Robinson, 35, of Norden-road, Bamford, Rochdale, said: "It was just an experiment in tracing air currents.

"When I sent up the balloons— ... at 5d. each from a ... ught the matter ... ent."

Flying Saucers make news –
and pictures! *Top left:*
Photograph of a UFO
taken by Giampiero
Monguzzi in the Bernina
Mountains, July 1952, and
(*top right*) a Saucer spotted
over Pedrada Gava in
South America the same
year

The newspaper reports
are from the *Daily Mail*,
August 1954 and the
Daily Mirror, March 1957

Centre: A sketch of a
saucer seen by Ronald
Wildman near Dunstable,
February 1962

Below: A space craft
hovering near High Bridge,
New Jersey, in 1956

Perhaps the most interesting account during this year, from our point of view, was the incident on 29 June 1954 when the pilots, crew and passengers of a BOAC stratocruiser saw several UFOs as they were crossing the Atlantic. The plane was flying at 19,000 feet on the New York to London route, via Goose Bay and Shannon, when suddenly the calm and uneventful flight was dramatically changed, as investigator John Carnell later reported:

> A weird collection of objects appeared through a break in the cloud cover, moving on a parallel course to the strato-cruiser at an estimated distance of four miles. A large shape-changing object, appearing rather like a swarm of bees, but solid, was accompanied by six small manoeuverable discs. The pilot reported to control and a fighter plane took off. When 15 miles away, the fighter radioed that he had the unknown objects, and the airliner, on his radar scope. At that instant the smaller objects moved into single file and appeared to enter the larger object, which then began to fade, disappearing as the fighter appeared overhead.[96]

The story did not end there, for, as Mr Carnell has said, during the rest of the year that same formation was to be seen several times again over various European countries and in America too. It is reports such as these that have led UFO investigators to the conclusion that there is probably more than just a single saucer-shaped type of craft, and that they probably come in a variety of different shapes and have differing capabilities of speed and manoeuvrability. As Jeremy Pascall has written, 'One should never assume that all the craft come from the same source, this is indicated by the myriad designs that are observed. Could, one is asked, the frequent reports of cigar-shaped objects be mother-crafts from which smaller shuttle vehicles exit?'

Theories as to the origin of the saucers have been almost as varied and numerous as the sightings themselves. A decade ago both the moon and Mars were proposed as their home bases in lengthy and well-argued books (Harold T. Wilkins's *Flying Saucers on the Moon* and the previously mentioned work by Cedric Allingham), while more recent theorists such as Brinsley Le Poer Trench have suggested that they may originate from inside the earth itself – being the means of transport of a super race who dwell there. Desmond Leslie, in contrast, believes that they could be the handiwork of the Atlanteans, who built them to flee the deluge and watch over us from their new home somewhere in the stars. Commenting on this area of speculation, that most rational of astronomers Patrick Moore has said: 'It is always dangerous to be too dogmatic, and one certainly cannot deny the possibility that the earth might be visited by extra-terrestrial beings: after all, life is probably widespread in the universe. On the other hand, it seems as certain as anything can be that there is no intelligent life in our solar system, except on the Earth, so that the saucers would have to come from tremendous distances amounting to millions of millions of miles.'

Mr Moore is particularly fascinated by the appeal that flying saucers have for large numbers of people – and by the fact that many eminent figures, such as

Air Chief Marshal Lord Dowding and Professor Hermann Oberth, the V-1 pioneer, have joined the ranks of believers. 'It may well be', he argues, 'that the saucer cult has achieved its wide popularity largely because of our changing ideas about the Universe. . . . Yet, on the whole, it is likely that the main factor is the realisation that our civilisation hangs by a thread; the wisdom of more advanced races might save us, and there is a strong wish to believe that helpers are not far away.'

Like other authorities in space research, he has been intrigued by the rise to prominence of the school of speculators who argue that much that was miraculous in our early history can be explained by the intervention of spacemen, and that these people have left their likenesses and handiwork throughout the nations of the world. 'It has been claimed,' he writes, 'that many of the miracles reported in the Bible are nothing more or less than rather garbled versions of interplanetary visitations. The book, 'Chariot of the Gods' (1967), based on the findings of Erich von Daniken, of Switzerland, claimed that spacemen from another world came to Earth not only in Biblical times, but even before. According to von Daniken, Egyptian mummies are simply time-travellers who have been "frozen" by means of techniques passed on to the pyramid-builders by the extraterrestrial beings.'[97]

Although it is unquestionably the books by von Daniken that have focused worldwide attention on this concept, he was not the first writer to put foward such ideas. In 1961, for instance, the distinguished Russian physicist Professor Agrest suggested that visitors from a distant star may have landed in the Near East in times gone by, leaving behind puzzling ancient structures. He cites the monuments of ancient art in the French Sahara with pictures of 'round head' figures which could be images of spacemen, as well as the ancient religious traditions that speak of 'gods' and 'sons of gods' who descended to earth, and Enoch who was taken alive to Heaven, all of which might be considered references to the same category of events. Professor Agrest also makes a particular point about certain ancient scientific treatises that seem to contain more than would be expected from a primitive state of knowledge and might reflect fragments of early teachings once handed to earthmen by the 'visitors' and preserved in an incomplete form.

Pioneer work has also been done in this field by the Briton Brinsley Le Poer Trench, who has suggested that the angels described in the Bible could have been men from space. According to him, the Bible also provides evidence that the 'armies of God' were an extraterrestrial expedition coming from outer space, and he quotes from Isaiah 13: 'I have commanded my sanctified ones, I have also called my mighty ones for mine anger, even them that rejoice in my highness. They came from a far country, from the end of heaven, even the Lord, and the weapons of his indignation, to destroy the whole land.' In his book *The Flying Saucer Story* Mr Le Poer Trench details many of the very earliest sightings of flying saucers, including a report on an Egyptian papyrus dating from the reign of Thutmose III (about 1504–1450 BC), of the visit to the land of a fleet of 'fire circles'; of the traditional beliefs of the

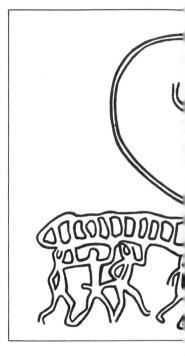

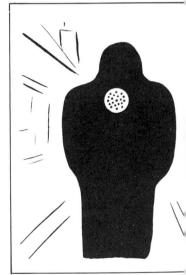

Top: Professor Agreat's sketch of the Sahara 'spacemen'.

Above: The four-foot high creature seen by Ernest Suddards in Bradford, Yorkshire, in August 1955

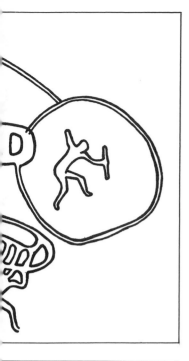

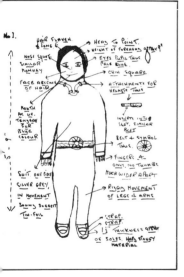

Above: Sketch of the flying saucer occupant encountered by Arthur Bryant in January 1966, illustration from *The Scoriton Mystery* by Eileen Buckle

Hopi Indians of Arizona and several other tribes that once 'gods' came down from the skies; and the famous Biblical account in Ezekiel of a spacecraft landing by the River Chebar. Mr Le Poer Trench goes on, 'My native country, Ireland, has more than its share of space visitors. There is the story of Cuchulain who defeated his foes in flying chariots. All over the world, in fact, there are the same stories handed down from ancient times of people who came from the skies. Ancient Egypt, India, Japan, China, Scandinavia, Ireland, the Americas, and many other lands, all tell of days when the "gods" trod this Earth of ours. Since time immemorial we have not been alone.'

Mr Le Poer Trench's view has been taken a stage further by Kenneth Huer, a former lecturer in astronomy at the Hayden Planetarium, who believes the space people may still be among us today. Writing in his book *Men of Other Planets* (1951) he says: 'If there have been guests from other worlds, we may be their descendants. It is possible that aeons ago our ancestors came from outer space as whole beings in space ships. There may even be planetarians in our society today – men of other planets may have been clever enough to take up the language and adopt the customs of the country in which they landed. They could be here in great numbers, but we would be unconscious of their presence. Or they may be here in such extraordinary forms as to be unrecognisable.' Mr Huer has received what some people consider a vindication of his statement in the form of reports of 'men in black' who have contacted saucer eye-witnesses. The more sceptical claim that if these people are not mere figments of the imagination, they might just be government officers trying to hush the whole business up!

Another American, the nuclear physicist Stanton T. Friedman, accepting that men from space may have visited earth, has been posing the question as to why, and has come up with a variety of reasons. Writing in his paper *Flying Saucers and Physics* (1974) he suggests that earth may be a rare supply depot for heavy metals and water, or that a visit to this planet might serve as a 'field trip for students to learn about primitive societies, uncontrolled weather, unmodified geological structures, countries at war, the slaughter of animals for food, and the absence of planetary control of language, birth, diseases and development'. He adds that 'Because of their advanced knowledge of planetary catastrophes such as magnetic pole tilting, supernova explosions, massive earthquakes, these space people may have sent a number of observational teams to gather data of what happens and how we handle it.'

Whether or not we accept the viewpoints of men like Huer and Friedman, they do represent the important change of heart that has taken place among scientists: they are now accepting the idea that there may after all be something in 'all this UFO nonsense', as it has been described. Dr Carl Sagan, the energetic and articulate NASA astronomer, probably best demonstrated this change when he was able to stand up before a meeting of the American Astronautical Society and tell an appreciative audience that 'The earth may have been visited by various galactic civilisations many times (possibly in the order of ten thousand) during geological time. It is not out of the question that artifacts of

High speed photograph of a saucer over Ireland

these visits still exist, or even that some kind of base is maintained (possibly automatically) within the solar system to provide continuity for successive expeditions.'[98] The British Astronomer Sir Fred Hoyle is of a like mind, and has suggested the possibility that 'a great intergalactic communications network exists but that we are like a settler in the wilderness who as yet has no telephone'.[99] Today, it would seem, the man of science is happy to join up with the so often derided UFO researcher in the quest for the truth about these phenomena in our skies.

It was the distinguished science fiction writer Arthur C. Clarke who pointed out recently that 'Any sufficiently advanced technology would appear indistinguishable from magic.'[100] And Flying Saucers, like so many of the other topics we have studied in this book, seem at first sight to have elements of magic about them. However, now, splendidly, what has happened is that we no longer automatically dismiss anything that smacks of the mysterious – denouncing and even punishing those who advocate the acceptance of such things – but approach them objectively, armed with all the sophisticated techniques of science and technology at our disposal. No longer are we afraid of what might prove to be the real truth of even our most ancient mysteries.

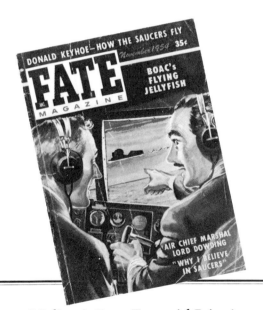

'I Believe in Extra-Terrestrial Beings'
Air Chief Marshal Lord Dowding writing in FATE magazine, November 1954

I HAVE never seen a "Flying Saucer," and yet I believe that they exist. I have never seen Australia and yet I believe that Australia also exists. My belief in both cases is based upon cumulative evidence in such quantity that, for me at any rate, it brings complete conviction.

More than 10,000 sightings have been reported, the majority of which cannot be accounted for by any "scientific" explanation, e.g., that they are hallucinations, the effects of light refraction, meteors, wheels falling from aeroplanes, and the like.

No earthly materials that we know of could be forced through the air at such speed without getting too hot to allow human occupants to exist. The accelerations which they develop in starting, changing course, and stopping would also make human life as we know it, impossible.

I say then that I am convinced that these objects do exist and that they are not manufactured by any nation on earth. I can therefore see no alternative to accepting the theory that they come from some extra-terrestrial source.

Please do not tell me that scientists affirm that life is not possible on other planets. They assume that "life" must necessarily exist in earth-type bodies. But it is only reasonable to suppose that bodies would be conditioned to the physical conditions existing on each planet.

Now that is as far as my "convictions" take me: beyond this my ideas are frankly speculative. The principal questions which arise are: Where do these objects come from? And what are the motives of the occupants in visiting the Earth's atmosphere?

I think that we must resist the tendency to assume that they all come from the same planet, or that they are all actuated by similar motives. It might be that visitors from one planet wished to help us in our evolution from the basis of a higher level to which they had attained.

Another planet might send an expedition to ascertain what have been these terrible explosions which they have observed, and to prevent us from discommoding other people besides ourselves by the new toys with which we are so light-heartedly playing.

Other visitors might have come bent solely on scientific discovery and might regard us with the dispassionate aloofness with which we might regard insects found beneath an upturned stone.

If I say that I believe that the majority of our visitors are actuated by friendly and helpful motives, I cannot produce the same volume of evidence in support of my opinion as I have done for the physical reality of the Saucers; but the fragmentary and uncorroborated evidence which I have is reinforced by the reasonability, if not the probability, of the idea that, if the inhabitants of other planets are so far ahead of us in making use of the (to us) unknown forces of nature, they may well be equally far ahead of us in spiritual evolution, and may have better methods of spreading their wisdom than by killing those who disagree with them.

It seems possible that for the first time in recorded history intelligible communication on the physical level may become possible between the earth and other planets of the solar system.

Such a prospect is epochmaking in the literal sense of the word, and we should be guilty of criminal folly if we were to do anything to hinder a contact which may well bring untold blessings to a distraught humanity.

Flying Saucer photographed
by Howard Menger in
New Jersey in 1956

NOTES

Chapter I

1. Plato, *The Dialogues (Critias)*.
2. *Records of the Royal Society of London for the Year 1692*.
3. Cotton Mather, *Wonders of the Invisible World* (Boston, 1692).
4. Captain John Symmes, quoted in *Atlantic Monthly Magazine*, May 1973.
5. ibid.
6. Richard M. Johnson, quoted by Marshall B. Gardner, *A Journey to the Earth's Interior* (private publication, 1913; reprinted Illinois, 1920).
7. Dr Willy Ley, quoted by Eric Norman, *This Hollow Earth* (New York, 1972).
8. Edward Bulwer Lytton, *The Coming Race* (London, 1871).
9. Gunther Rosenberg, quoted by Ellic Howe, *Astrology and Psychological Warfare During World War II* (London, 1967).
10. Herman Rauschning, quoted by Louis Pauwels and Jacques Bergier, *Morning of the Magicians* (Paris, 1960).
11. William Reed, *Phantom of the Poles* (New York, 1906).
12. Rear-Admiral R. E. Byrd, quoted by Raymond Bernard, *The Hollow Earth* (New York, 1969).
13. ibid.
14. *Flying Saucers Magazine*, December 1959.
15. Olaf Jansen, quoted in *The Smoky God*, presented by Willis George Emerson (Los Angeles, 1908).

Chapter II

16. Hamish MacInnes writing in the *Observer*, 4 November 1963.
17. ibid., 18 November 1963.
18. J. F. Schofield, *Survey of the Recent Prehistory of Southern Rhodesia* (London, 1942).
19. L. Sprague de Camp, *Citadels of Mystery* (London, 1975).
20. James O'Connell, *The Life of James F. O'Connell, The Pacific Adventurer* (New York, 1853).
21. Thor Heyerdahl, *Archaeology of Easter Island* (London, 1961).
22. Charles Berlitz, *Mysteries from Forgotten Worlds* (New York, 1972).
23. Andrew Tomas, *From Legend to Discovery* (Paris, 1972).

Chapter III

24. Dr Helge Ingstad, *Westward to Vinland* (New York, 1969).

25. Torhallur Vilmundarson, *Reflections on the Vinland Map* (Oslo, 1966).
26. André Norton, 'Ghost Tour', in *Witchcraft and Sorcery*, January 1971.
27. Quoted by Esmond Wright, 'The British in America', in the *Observer Magazine*, 28 June 1975.

Chapter IV

28. E. W. MacKie, *Stone Circles: For Savages or Savants?* (London, 1968).
29. E. W. MacKie, 'The Inner Circle', in the *Sunday Times*, 15 April 1973.
30. Gerald S. Hawkins, *Beyond Stonehenge* (New York, 1973). See also *Stonehenge Decoded* by the same author (New York, 1965).
31. John Aubrey, *Miscellanies* (London, 1696).

Chapter V

32. Aristotle, *On Marvellous Things Heard*.
33. William H. Babcock, *Legendary Islands of the Atlantic* (New York, 1922).
34. Quoted by the *New York Times*, December 1901.
35. Quoted by L. Sprague de Camp, *Lost Continents* (New York, 1954).
36. Ernst Haekel, *Erdegeschichte* (Berlin, 1887).
37. O. G. S. Crawford, 'Lyonnes', in *Antiquity*, vol. I, 1927.
38. Quoted by Christopher Grey, *The Lost Land of Lyonesse* (London, 1974).
39. ibid.

Chapter VI

40. Sir Martin Frobisher, *Three Voyages*, ed. E. Stefansson (London, 1938).
41. Quoted by L. Powys, *The Life of Henry Hudson: Navigator and Discoverer* (London, 1927).
42. Quoted by Rupert T. Gould, *Oddities* (London, 1928).
43. The *Nautical Magazine*, 1893.
44. Quoted in *The Transactions of the Royal Hydrographical Society of Madrid* (Madrid, 1809).
45. James Weddell, *Voyage Towards the South Pole* (London, 1825).
46. Rupert T. Gould, op. cit.
47. ibid.
48. Quoted by Elliot O'Donnell, 'Phantom Islands of the Atlantic', in *Prediction*, June 1946.
49. Rupert T. Gould, op. cit.
50. ibid.
51. *Admiralty Reports for the Year 1859*, Admiralty Records Office.
52. ibid.
53. Quoted by Lord Christensen, *Such is the Antarctic* (London, 1935).

Chapter VII

54. Quoted in *Arthur Machen: Memories and Impressions*, ed. Father Brocard Sewell (London, 1960).

55. Quoted by Odette Tchernine, *The Yeti* (London, 1970).

56. Ivor T. Sanderson, 'Wudewasa: The Furry Men of Europe', in *Fate* magazine, 1964.

57. ibid.

58. Quoted by Bernard Heuvelmans, *On the Track of Unknown Animals* (New York, 1958).

59. Quoted by Lance Robbins, 'Wyoming's Mystery Mummy', in *Exploring the Unknown*, May 1965.

Chapter VIII

60. C. K. Howard Bury, *Mount Everest, the Reconnaissance* (London, 1922).

61. ibid.

62. Eric Shipton, quoted by Odette Tchernine, op. cit.

63. Quoted by Ivor T. Sanderson, *Abominable Snowman: Legend Come to Life* (New York, 1961).

64. *Illustrated London News*, 27 March 1954.

65. *Daily Telegraph*, 18 July 1973.

66. *The Times*, 28 July 1973.

67. Quoted by Dan Hunter, with Rene Dahinden, *Sasquatch* (Toronto, 1973).

68. Quoted by Ivor T. Sanderson, *Abominable Snowman: Legend Come to Life* (New York, 1961).

Chapter IX

69. Quoted by Constance Whyte, *The Loch Ness Monster* (Inverness, 1951).

70. Tim Dinsdale, *Loch Ness Monster* (London, 1961).

71. Quoted by Constance Whyte, *More Than a Legend* (London, 1957).

72. Quoted by Rupert T. Gould, *The Loch Ness Monsters and Others* (London, 1934).

73. Quoted by F. W. Holiday, *The Great Orm of Loch Ness* (London, 1969).

74. Quoted by Constance Whyte, op. cit.

75. *Daily Mirror*, 11 December 1975.

76. Quoted by Peter Costello, *In Search of Lake Monsters* (London, 1974).

77. ibid.

78. Quoted by Rupert T. Gould, *The Case for the Sea Serpent* (London, 1930).

78. Quoted by Peter Costello, op. cit.

80. ibid.

81. ibid.

82. Quoted by Rupert T. Gould, *The Loch Ness Monsters and Others* (Inverness, 1951).

83. Quoted by Peter Costello, op. cit.

84. Quoted in *Victoria Daily Times*, 2 December 1933.

85. Quoted in *Nature*, January 1954.

86. Quoted by W. Savile-Kent, *The Great Barrier Reef of Australia* (London, 1893).

87. Quoted in *Time* magazine, June 1925.

Chapter X

88. Quoted in the *Idaho Statesman*, June 1947.

89. Quoted by Brinsley Le Poer Trench, *The Flying Saucer Story* (London, 1966).

90. Quoted by Harold T. Wilkins, *Flying Saucers on the Moon* (London, 1954).

91. Quoted by Brinsley Le Poer Trench, op. cit.

92. Charles Bowen, 'Flying Saucers', in *Fate and Fortune*, Issue 7, 1974.

93. Jeremy Pascall, 'Who Believes in UFOs?', in *Club* magazine, 1971.

94. ibid.

95. Charles Bowen, 'Flying Saucers', op. cit.

96. John Carnell, 'BOAC's Flying Jelly Fish', in *Fate* magazine, November 1954.

97. Patrick Moore, 'Flying Saucers', in *Man, Myth and Magic*, No. 36, 1970.

98. Quoted in *Time* magazine, 21 January 1974.

99. Sir Fred Hoyle, quoted by Ralph Blum, 'UFOs: No One's Laughing Any More', in *Time* magazine, January 1975.

100. *Newsweek*, 4 August 1974.

SELECT
BIBLIOGRAPHY

ADAMSKI, George and LESLIE, Desmond, *Flying Saucers Have Landed*, London 1953.

ARNOLD, Kenneth, *The Coming of the Saucers*, Wisconsin 1952.

BABCOCK, William H., *Legendary Islands of the Atlantic*, New York 1922.

BERLITZ, Charles, *The Mystery of Atlantis*, New York 1959.

—— *The Bermuda Triangle*, New York 1974, London 1975.

BERNARD, Dr Raymond, *The Hollow Earth*, New York 1969.

BOLAND, Charles, *They All Discovered America*, New York 1961.

BORD, Janet and Colin, *Mysterious Britain*, London 1972.

CHURCHWARD, James, *The Lost Continent of Mu*, London 1931.

COSTELLO, Peter, *In Search of Lake Monsters*, London 1974.

DANIKEN, Erich von, *Chariots of the Gods?*, London 1967.

—— *Return to the Stars*, London 1970.

—— *Gold of the Gods*, London 1973.

DAVIDSON, Basil, *Lost Cities of Africa*, London 1959.

—— *Old Africa Rediscovered*, London 1961.

DE CAMP, L. Sprague, *Lost Continents*, New York 1954.

—— *Ancient Ruins and Archeology*, New York 1964.

DINSDALE, Tim, *Loch Ness Monster*, London 1961.

DONNELLY, Ignatius, *Atlantis: The Antediluvian World*, New York 1882.

ENTERLINE, James Robert, *Viking America*, New York 1972.

GALANOPOULOS, Angelous and BACON, Edward, *Atlantis*, London 1969.

GARDNER, Marshall B., *A Journey to the Earth's Interior*, New York 1913.

GATHORNE-HARDY, G. M., *The Norse Discoverers of America*, London 1921.

GOULD, Charles, *Mythical Monsters*, London 1886.

GOULD, Rupert T., *Oddities*, London 1928.

—— *The Case for the Sea Serpent*, London 1930.

—— *The Loch Ness Monster and Others*, London 1934.

GREEN, John, *On the Track of the Sasquatch*, British Columbia 1968.

HADINGHAM, Evan, *Circles and Standing Stones*, London 1975.

HAWKINS, Gerald S., *Stonehenge Decoded*, New York 1965, London (paperback) 1970.

—— *Beyond Stonehenge*, New York and London 1973.

HEUVELMANS, Bernard, *On the Trail of Unknown Animals*, New York 1965.

HEYERDAHL, Thor, *The Kon-Tiki Expedition*, tr. F. H. Lyon, London 1950.

—— *The Archeology of Easter Island*, London 1961.

HOLIDAY, F. W., *The Great Orm of Loch Ness*, London 1969.

—— *The Dragon and the Disc*, London 1973.

HUNTER, Don and DAHINDEN, René, *Sasquatch*, Toronto 1973.

INGSTAD, Dr Helga, *Westward to Vinland*, London 1969.

IZZARD, Ralph, *The Abominable Snowman Adventure*, London 1954.

LETHBRIDGE, T. E., *Gogmagog, The Buried Gods*, London 1975.

—— *The Legend of the Sons of God*, London 1972.

LOCKYER, Sir Norman, *Stonehenge and Other British Stone Monuments Astronomically Considered*, London 1909.

LORENZEN, Coral E., *The Shadow of the Unknown*, New York 1970.

LUCE, J. V., *The End of Atlantis*, London 1969.

MACINNES, Hamish, *Journey to the Lost World*, London 1975.

MORRISON, S. E., *The European Discovery of America*, London 1971.

NAPIER, John, *Bigfoot: Yeti and Sasquatch in Myth and Reality*, London 1972.

NORMAN, Eric, *This Hollow Earth*, New York 1972.

OSENDOWSKI, Ferdinand, *Beasts, Man and Gods*, London 1923.

PATTERSON, Roger, *Do Abominable Snowmen of America Really Exist?*, Yakima 1966.

PAUWELS, Louis and BERGIER, Jacques, *The Eternal Man*, London 1972.

PLATO, *Timaeus* and *Critias*, 4th century B.C.

REED, William, *The Phantom of the Poles*, New York 1906.

ROOSEVELT, Theodore, *The Wilderness Hunter*, New York 1893.

SANDERSON, Ivan T., *Abominable Snowman: Legend Come to Life*, Philadelphia 1973.

SCHOFIELD, J. F., *Survey of the Recent Prehistory of South Africa*, London 1942.

SPENCE, Lewis, *History of Atlantis*, London 1925.

—— *The Problem of Atlantis*, London 1926.

STUKELEY, William, *Stonehenge, A Temple Restor'd to the British Druids*, London 1740.

—— *Abury, A Temple of the British Druids*, London 1743.

SYMMES, Captain John, *Symmes' Theory of Concentric Spheres and Polar Voids*, New York 1826.

TCHERNINE, Odette, *In Pursuit of the Abominable Snowman*, New York 1971.

—— *The Yeti*, London 1971.

THOM, Professor Alexander, *Megalithic Sites in Britain*, Oxford 1967.

—— *Megalithic Lunar Observatories*, Oxford 1971.

TRENCH, Brinsley Le Poer, *The Flying Saucer Story*, London 1966.

—— *Secret of the Ages: UFOs from Inside the Earth*, London 1974.

WEBB, J, F. (tr.), *Voyage of St Brendan*, London 1965.

WELLARD, James, *The Search for Lost Worlds*, London 1975.

WHYTE, Constance, *The Loch Ness Monster*, Edinburgh 1951.

—— *More than a Legend*, Edinburgh 1957.

WITCHELL, Nicholas, *The Loch Ness Story*, Lavenham 1974.

INDEX

References in italics refer to pages on which illustrations appear

Notes:
i) Keep the run-up down to no more than 5 or 6 metres.
ii) Bag holders are needed on each bag. Give them a spot on which to replace after the tackle.
iii) Change holders after every round.
iv) Remember to instruct that bags be released by holders on impact of tackle.

I like to use the 5 m touch-line. By placing the bags just inside the line, there is incentive for every tackler to lift/drive the bags back over the line…

Variations:
Introduce several items…
1 = tackle. 2 = maul off another player. 3 = Fall and pick up. 4 = tackle again…

10 – CONTINUITY SKILLS

A New Zealand Warmer…
2 balls. 4 Teams of any size.

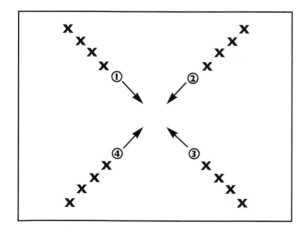

First man from 1 – switch with first from 3.
First from 2 switch with first from 4.
Keep it going as relay.

Variations can include:
i) Close switch,
ii) ball on deck in middle for pick up,
iii) roll ball for fielding,
iv) spin pass &c.